T0293973

Letter ~~~~ Daughter

---

*Words of wisdom, advice and
lessons on life from mothers*

EDITED BY THERESA TAN

Marshall Cavendish
Editions

Text © individual contributors as credited in each work
© 2020 Marshall Cavendish International (Asia) Private Limited

Published in 2020 by Marshall Cavendish Editions
An imprint of Marshall Cavendish International

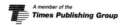
A member of the
Times Publishing Group

All rights reserved

No part of this publication may be reproduced, stored in a retrieval system or transmit-
ted, in any form or by any means, electronic, mechanical, photocopying, recording
or otherwise, without the prior permission of the copyright owner. Requests for
permission should be addressed to the Publisher, Marshall Cavendish International
(Asia) Private Limited, 1 New Industrial Road, Singapore 536196. Tel: (65) 6213 9300
E-mail: genref@sg.marshallcavendish.com Website: www.marshallcavendish.com/genref

The publisher makes no representation or warranties with respect to the contents
of this book, and specifically disclaims any implied warranties or merchantability or
fitness for any particular purpose, and shall in no event be liable for any loss of profit
or any other commercial damage, including but not limited to special, incidental,
consequential, or other damages.

Other Marshall Cavendish Offices:
Marshall Cavendish Corporation, 800 Westchester Ave, Suite N-641, Rye Brook,
NY 10573, USA • Marshall Cavendish International (Thailand) Co Ltd, 253 Asoke,
16th Floor, Sukhumvit 21 Road, Klongtoey Nua, Wattana, Bangkok 10110, Thailand
• Marshall Cavendish (Malaysia) Sdn Bhd, Times Subang, Lot 46, Subang Hi-Tech
Industrial Park, Batu Tiga, 40000 Shah Alam, Selangor Darul Ehsan, Malaysia

Marshall Cavendish is a registered trademark of Times Publishing Limited

National Library Board, Singapore Cataloguing-in-Publication Data

Names: Tan, Theresa, 1967- editor.
Title: Letter to my daughter : words of wisdom, advice and lessons on life from
      mothers / edited by Theresa Tan.
Description: Singapore : Marshall Cavendish Editions, 2020.
Identifiers: OCN 1184754848 | ISBN 978-981-4893-65-7 (paperback)
Subjects: LCSH: Mothers—Correspondence. | Mothers and daughters. |
      Women—Conduct of life.
Classification: DDC 306.8743—dc23

Printed in Singapore

Cover design by Adithi Khandadai

Letter to my Daughter

This book is dedicated to all mothers and future mothers, in the hope that these shared experiences will inspire and shape your own parenting journey.

Contents

Foreword   9
THERESA TAN

PART 1: LESSONS FROM MY DAUGHTER

How My Three Daughters Made Me Who I Am   14
AMY POON

Become Women Who Make A Difference   23
KAREN TAN

In Appreciation Of My Daughters   30
NG CHOONG SAN

When I Was 17   36
PETRINA KOW

Lessons My Four Daughters Taught Me   45
DAWN SIM

My Motherhood Experiment   53
CHIONG XIAO TING

PART 2: WHEN LIFE THROWS YOU LEMONS

The Incredible Story Of Why We Moved To New Zealand   62
ADLENA WONG

Triumphing Over life's Challenges   75
KALTHUM AHMAD

How You Became My Daughter   87
LIN XIUZHEN

Mommy's Running Chronicles   93
LORETTA URQUHART

To Be A Mother Is The Best Decision I Ever Made 105
Dawn Lee

PART 3: THE BABY GIRL GROWS UP

Humility, Grit And The Family Business 116
Janet Goh

Face Your Future Bravely 124
Jenny Wee

A Letter To My Daughter Going Away To University 133
Sangegta Mukchand

A Mother's Emotional Odyssey 142
Zalina Gazali

The Importance Of Identity & A Good Red Lipstick 152
Cynthia Chew

PART 4: WISDOM FOR THE REST OF YOUR LIFE

A Letter From Your "Fun" Tiger Mom 164
Paige Parker

The Important Things In Life 175
Shaan Moledina-Lim

Everything I Want You To Be 188
Landy Chua

How To Be Courageous 197
Jennifer Heng

Lessons In Love And Life 208
Yen Chua

Foreword

Theresa Tan

My dearest daughters, Bethany and Becca

I said yes to this project because it's something I've always wanted to do: write you each a letter at various milestones in your—and my—lives. But, like many of the ladies here, I've been putting it off, because there's always another fire to fight or sourdough to bake (yes, your procrastination genes came from me). So this project was, quite honestly, a gift to me.

The relationship between a Mommy and her little girl is a very special, and often very complex one. We all see ourselves in you, as I do in your bursts of creativity, from writing to fashion to embroidery, Beth; in your cartooning and endless doodling, Becca. We also dread seeing you go through all the pain we once went through: the failures, the disappointments, the heartbreaks. As much as we want to protect you from them, we also know, ultimately, we have to let you live your life so you can become the person you are meant to be. But that may not necessarily stop us freaking out and screaming at you—primarily because we've made the same mistakes and we'd rather you didn't.

Bethany, Becca and Theresa are fans of the Harry Porter series of films.

When I looked for the most interesting mothers of daughters for this book, I gave each of them a blank slate to write what they most wanted to say to their daughters. Every mother is different. Every daughter is different. So you will read letters of joy—a mother who spent every weekend and holiday sitting and doing homework with her learning-challenged daughter now celebrates that same daughter's success as an artist. You will read deeply honest, confessional letters—a mother who lived through incredibly difficult years, who has now plucked her daughters and relocated far away to start afresh, away from the pressures of Singapore living. You will read inspiring letters from mothers who have survived adversities like cancer and divorce. You will also read letters of gratitude from mothers to their daughters, and letters of hope.

Each of these letters is a precious gem. I know every one of these mothers poured their hearts and souls into what they wrote. I pray that as their daughters read these letters—now, or for some, when they grow older—that they will come to know their mothers better, understand them and love them for who they are.

As for you, my daughters, this book is also my gift to you. One day you will be mothers yourselves—I look forward to being a grandmother. I hope, as you read this, you will gain wisdom, knowledge, understanding, inspiration and encouragement to be a strong, courageous person who makes this world a better place, wherever you may go.

I love you both with all my heart.

Mom

THERESA TAN is a writer, editor, screenwriter and a playwright. She has had over 30 years of creative editorial experience, including being a writer for *8 Days*, and the editor of *Female*, *ELLE*, *Tiger Tales* and *Vanilla*. She has also written columns for *The Straits Times* and *DARE* magazine. Theresa co-founded WORD Agency in 2006, and the agency provides writing and editing services to corporate and government clients. Theresa has also worked on books, including the Autism Resource Centre's 20th anniversary book, *Making a Difference Together*. She also authored her own book *A Clean Breast*, based on her journey through breast cancer. Theresa is the mother of three children, aged between 14 and 21, who are her pride, joy and fountain of youth.

Part 1

LESSONS FROM MY DAUGHTER

"My daughter introduced me to myself."
—Beyoncé

How My Three Daughters Made Me Who I am

Amy Poon

To my dear daughters,

I wish you all to know that I love all of you equally and unconditionally, even though you may not think so. The three of you are so different in your own special ways and I have learnt so much from each of you. The precious lessons you have taught me during your various milestones have made me who am I today. And the lessons are still ongoing.

Xiang, your arrival into our family made me appreciate my mother, your Mama—with whom I had been at loggerheads since I was a teenager—much more. Your birth bridged the gap between me and my sisters, especially, your Aunty Wendy with whom I was constantly competing for Mama's attention and approval which I never got. Their love for you healed me and made me a better daughter and sister. I cannot thank you enough for that.

Your learning difficulties led me on a journey of searching for therapies to help you cope within our education system.

That continuous search brought me through many self-help courses, and finally to obtaining a degree in psychology and a Master's degree in counseling. Most importantly, you led me to a career that has enabled me to help many other children with learning difficulties, many of them more challenging that yours.

Growing up, you were—and still are—very sensitive and receptive to the thoughts of others, always accommodating to ideas and suggestions. You attended every class that I enrolled you in, from tap dance and ballet to abacus—even Latin dancing. I knew you disliked it but you accommodated Dad and I. When it came to studies and homework, what took others a short time to complete, you took a whole day. My heart went out to you when you did not have time to play as much as the other children did. But you were the slow and steady results producer.

Despite your learning challenges, your persistence and grit in wanting to do your best in a top school when you could have chosen a less competitive school environment, made me more determined to support you in your love for art and to see you succeed. You took ownership of your career in art and I am so proud of you. At each of your exhibitions that I attend, I always stand in awe and am mesmerized by your works, and the effort and depth of your processes that make each piece so spectacular.

More importantly, I love you for your altruistic nature. No matter how busy your schedule is, you will always make time for anyone who is in need of your help. Your gentle demeanour makes you approachable and easy to talk to, and you are always courteous to people around you. Do stay this way but never let anyone take advantage of you. Learn to say no, if you feel that you are unable to extend your help.

Xiang, I am sorry that I was a "Tiger Mum" to you. I only realized that after reading Amy Chua's book in 2011. But, you thanked me for being one because you felt that I was somewhat instrumental in helping you arrive at doing what you are most passionate about: art. I was and will always be your biggest supporter in everything that you do. Of course, now your next biggest supporter is, Chris, your significant other.

Xiang, I am so grateful that you are my eldest daughter because, despite many hurdles, you have risen above all adversities, leading by example and paving the way for your sisters to follow your grit and persistence.

***

To my second daughter, Yuan, my little monkey who was always mischievous and hard to keep up with. Since you could walk, your favorite past-time was climbing up window grills and hiding behind the drapes. On rainy days, we would find you soaking wet, playing and drinking rain water from the rain gutter. That was how we discovered you had a mighty strong gut.

From a very young age, you were never shy with strangers. You were courageous and confident from the time you attended a Montessori playschool at age 4. You insisted in wearing your cousin's old SCGS (Singapore Chinese Girls' School) uniform to playschool every day, with not a care in the world. Even the other parents found you amusing. I loved how you enjoyed attending the notorious Chen Lao Shi's grueling Chinese writing classes when you were only five, and diligently hand in your *ci zi* (Chinese writing practice) week after week. You were so observant of everything around you. You managed to calculate how much Chen Lao Shi earned a month, you were barely six. You were competitive from young and chose gymnastics for your co-curricular activity. I thought you might give up, but you did not. You persisted and competed in interschool gymnastics competitions. I applaud you for your persistence and courage.

You were independent, confident and you knew exactly what you needed to achieve the good academic results that you wanted. I was in awe of how organized you were in planning your tuition classes, CCA and school curriculum. From you, I learnt to be more organized since I had to multitask, managing your and Xiang's classes. I enjoyed my Yuan-and-Mummy-only times, when we would have lunch together or tea together. I loved being able to give you full attention even though you were mostly eating. I miss those moments and I wish I had had more time for you then. When Qi Qi was born, you were the best sister, playmate and teacher every parent could wish for. On reaching home from school, you would read to her every day and play with her, and it was a joy to see how well you took on the role of big sister and teacher. Qi Qi had the best playmate with endless ideas, including pretend camping in the bedroom, with blankets and torch lights hanging from hangers and cupboard doors. I cannot thank you enough for helping to look after Qi Qi while I was busy focusing on helping Xiang with her school work.

I was so blessed that I did not have to worry about your academic achievements. You did all your own research and knew exactly what you needed to get the scholarship for university. Because you were so sure of the medical career you wanted, you worked hard towards achieving it, even though it took you eight years: four years in the University Scholars Programme (USP) at the National University of Singapore, and four more at Duke-NUS.

Inspired by your tenacity and determination, I felt courageous enough to embark on my own studies and I enjoyed studying together with you and your sisters. The dining table that turned into a messy study table full of books, especially during examinations left me with fond memories up to this day. I miss those nights of studying late into the night, ordering suppers from McDonalds at 1am. And to destress, you taught me to download Plants vs Zombies, and I enjoyed chasing Pokémon with you and your sisters. I learnt what it felt like to be addicted and more importantly, when to stop playing. We worked hard and we played hard. That was our motto.

Yuan, I thank you for being the middle child, so independent and steadfast in achieving your dreams. As a middle child myself, I grew up with low self-esteem but it is from you that I was able to realize my dream to pursue my Masters.

***

Dear Qi, you arrived on 31 December, when I had intended to go a New Year's Eve ball. You were six days too early. My first worry for you was school—you would be a year-end child in a class full of kids older than you.

My second worry was that I had just turned 41 and I was afraid that I would be mistaken as your grandmother when I send you to school. But you are the pure reason why I have stayed young at heart, and young in mind and body. I started learning about nutrition and supplements, how to stay fit and healthy. This has allowed me to enjoy growing old with you and your sisters. My greatest fear is to be a burden to all of you if I were unhealthy.

Qi Qi, you were such an easy baby to look after. Like Yuan, you were never afraid of strangers. Many of my friends remember you as the little girl carrying your plastic golf clubs confidently walking around the Singapore Island Country Club with your Dad on weekends, while I was at home accompanying Xiang as she completed her school homework. I did not know if you would be artsy like Xiang or more science-y like Yuan. But you loved to draw, sing and breakdance when you were only five. You carried around a CD of the band Blue and your favourite song was *One Love*. My, at such a young age!

You refused to attend play school and kindergarten, and it was only with much persuasion that you agreed to attended one year of Montessori before going to SCGS like your sisters. Strangely, as time passed, I had become quite chill about school since I had firsthand experience of Xiang's education at SCGS. I am so amazed to see how you picked up a liking for books after reading Harry Potter, and thereafter, you could always be seen with a book in your hand.

Another surprise from you was when you took part in the school Talentime contest. Even though the sound system broke down during your performance, you were composed and delivered your song unflinchingly. When you were only 14, your leadership and public-speaking qualities awed me, and I was so proud of you because public speaking was my greatest fear.

I am sorry that you had to give up your dreams of studying overseas because you knew we had limited finances. Your Dad and I were so proud of you when you worked hard to get yourself accepted in USP, which indicated a maturity and understanding that surpassed your young age.

You are such a joy to have and words cannot describe how proud I am of you. I applaud you for being proactive and resourceful, choosing to study Biomedical Engineering, even though you knew you had to put in a lot of effort. And you aced it. I am tearful as I think about how difficult it must have been for you—and yet you pressed on. Given the current COVID pandemic as I write this, I have noticed that you are versatile and adaptable in considering the pursuit of your PhD. I am so happy for you that you have been accepted to work on a one-year research at the School of Public Health, NUS. I am amazed at your determination and wish you the very best in your endeavours.

***

So in ending, what I wish to say is that I am so blessed to have you three girls, so different yet so similar in how you all set out to achieve your goals; how you have all persevered and ultimately arrived at the intended destination. Yes, I admit that I am a Tiger Mum in some ways and I apologize if I had been too hard on all of you. What I appreciate most about the three of you is that you are not afraid to challenge me and to point out my faults. Something I have learnt during the Circuit Breaker period is that, as a family, we are able to work out our differences and appreciate each other's weaknesses.

I like it, Yuan, when you sit me down to talk things out whenever you feel that I am being unreasonable. I am confident that in times of need, the three of you will there for each other. If I had a chance to do things differently, I would have studied psychology and counseling before giving birth to the three of you. I have learnt so much from each of you individually. From Xiang, I've learnt to be passionate in my work. From Yuan, I learnt to gather my facts and evidence before I say something. And from Qi Qi, I learnt to be more sensitive and cautious with my sweeping statements. As you have pointed out to me, words that are acceptable to my generation are not acceptable to yours. Thank you for being my teachers, girls.

Lastly, I am grateful to the three of you for helping me pull through our storms together—some felt more like tsunamis. I am so proud that I am a mother to you three wonderful, mature and thoughtful girls.

AMY POON was a housewife turned neuro feedback therapist and counselor with Lingguo Synpaz (previously known as Lingguo Brain Therapy Centre), where she provides clinical services in neuro feedback and counselling to children and adults with special needs, to bridge brain and behaviour through regulation of brain waves and self-control.

Prior to her career, she chose to be a stay-home mother after the birth of her first child. As she was raising three girls,

Amy Poon (first from left) with her three daughters.

she remained a keen learner and enrolled in NUS Regional Chinese Language Centre to study Chinese, and attended courses in hypnotherapy and neurolinguistic programming. Today, Amy is a Certified Hypnotherapy and NLP Practitioner.

Her penchant for learning led her to James Cook University, where she read Psychology and received a Master's degree in Guidance and Counselling. Her entrepreneurial spirit led her to embark on an online business five years ago, where she specialises in health and nutrition and is a sought-after speaker on how nutrition affects the mind and body. These days, she integrates neurofeedback therapy, nutrition and counseling in a multiprong approach for her clients. She attributes her success to her attitude towards lifelong learning and the constant upgrading of her skills.

Become Women Who Make A Difference

Karen Tan

Dearest Raym and Bahbayne

This letter took longer to write than I'd planned, having given up my laptop to Liv, and not having that much to write anymore, I had to deal with the desktop in the study, and it's taken me forever to figure out how to even get to opening a new document. I finally managed by messaging Rachel. It really is (not always, but often… well, maybe sometimes) funny how everything is in reverse now.

I'm sure you both must already notice how much more helpless I seem to be these days. My inability to grasp technology, my getting words mixed up, my getting cross for no reason (though the reasons are often quite clear in my head, "How come you don't geddit?"), my letting you both do things that I would normally have jumped up to do myself. I am older, more grumpy, more "more blur", more willing to give in, and to pass on. And it's really terrific that you've both worked together to get things done. Rachel, of course, always takes the lead, being nine years older places that responsibility automatically on you, I'm afraid. And Olivia has to take orders, as younger ones have to do. It's part of the family food system, and it's nice to see it coming together so well.

I always told myself that if I ever had children, I had to like them. Love is all very well, and pretty much part of the agreement, but liking is something else. I had to like being with my children, to like sitting quietly with them, or being boisterous with them; eating with them; scolding them; shopping with them; looking at them. Love has a nice way of smoothing raw bits over; liking requires an extra bit of effort to look at raw bits to fix them. Hence, the recently made-up saying (by me): "Because I love you, I won't tell you you're being horrible, but because I like you, I will." Discuss.

I still tell people that the only things I'm leaving you both (and yes, Liv, I know you hate it when I talk about death—sorry) are my vintage plates, the old Enid Blytons I found in Bras Basah Complex, and my yarn. My dresses and shoes too, of course, which is debatable, as Rachel's feet are already larger than mine, and neither of you really like my clothes. My scripts you can recycle, or maybe sell off as new, since I never wrote notes. And... that's it, really. That's all I have to pass to you girls. Gosh. Even I'm surprised.

I've got no money, really sorry about that. But you've both known always that being an actor has never resulted in a very large paycheck. I always chose the theatre over any other medium because I felt I could perform the best there. There is an honesty and truth in the theatre that you cannot find in film or TV. And one honest, brutal truth about theatre work is that you get paid very little. It's something your Papa and I knew and accepted years ago, and it's something you've grown accustomed to.

Still, it did hurt when I was between shows or cheques, and I wasn't able to buy you the nice meal you wanted, or the new book, or just a treat. But I learned that when I was honest and said I hadn't been paid yet, can you wait, the answer was always, "Oh, okay", with no sulking or questioning or anything. And soon enough, I would be paid, and the book/meal/treat was bought, and life continued. And I've come realise, truly, it's only money. "Money can earn", we always say, and in the end… it's only money.

So, girls, earning money is great, it really is! It is nice to have money to spend, and to splurge on others, to save up. Right now, I wish I had loads of it!

But the reality is, if you were both whiny and grumbled about how and why you couldn't have what you wanted, then no money can save you from what could become a blackhole in your personalities. (And here, I've replaced another word with "black".)

In the few times I was asked by your school to do a career talk to the leaving students, I always told them that It didn't matter how well they did, how many degrees they got, how much money they earned, it all meant nothing if they had the personality of a cockroach.

Hence, my wanting children that not only I would like, but that everyone else would too.

Hence, my always talking to you like you were people, even as babies. My always waiting for a response, always

Rachel (left) and Olivia (middle) with their mother, Karen (right).

watching to see what you did, how you reacted, what you said, how you felt. I will always ask how you are, because it's important for you to know how you feel about something, because then you will know how others feel too.

I always insist (though more patiently now, I hope) that you say what you feel, and not bottle it in, because I, of all people, know the damage of holding in anger, resentment, sadness, disappointment, deep despair. Yet, I can't and won't prevent you from feeling these things, because Life will continue to present them to you, and you will have to learn to recognise these visitors.

Hence, my hope and prayers are always that you will both become women who make a difference in people's lives. Because recognising these feelings, as well as joy, gratitude, peace, and happiness, can only create in you, hearts that are open to others, willing to listen, ready to help. This is something both the rich and poor can do, but I realise that having little money, and still being able to share and help, is something pretty special, and I hope you will experience this constantly.

Though I would prefer you to not experience abject poverty. Really. Please earn your keep. This is a very long-winded letter, and I'm glad I'm not writing it by hand.

Rachel and Olivia, I always have loads to say, and I would jump up in a jiffy and offer advice whenever I can. But I also brought you both up to be independent, and to take on whatever you have to on your own, and to complete tasks with your own skills.

So, I think the most important thing I can say to you both is to Never Be Afraid to Do the Right Thing.

Here's a list (because you know how much I love, and live by, lists):

- Never be afraid to give your seat to an old person.
- Never be afraid to stop someone kicking a kitten.
- Never be afraid to say you don't know the answer.
- Never be afraid to ask for help.
- Never be afraid to give help.
- Never be afraid to say "No", especially if it's against what you believe in, even if everyone else says Yes.
- Never be afraid to say "Yes", when you know it's the right thing to do. Always greet your friends' parents when you see them.
- Always say hullo to older people in the lift or shops.
- Always greet people before you eat.
- Always say "Thank You".
- Always answer in full sentences, even when you don't feel like it.

- Always smile at service staff because, really, their jobs can be pretty miserable. Don't be a keyboard warrior—go out and actively change the small things around you.
- Don't be a bully, online or physically.
- Don't let your friends be bullies.
- Don't be bullied—take many deep breaths, and say/type "No"
- Don't let the world overwhelm you. Always have integrity.
- Always have courage.
- Always have humility.

Wah. Such a nice way to end a letter.

It's funny to be writing to you both like this, because the recent Circuit Breaker ensured that we saw each other, all day, every day, for six weeks. Plus, we always WhatsApp each other, even while in the same room.

I suppose this is a letter that shouldn't end, because my life with you both is still going on, and this letter is really a timely reminder to myself that I have been so, so, so blessed to be a mother to you both. That as much as mothers take all the credit, they won't be who they are without the children, and if anyone gives me credit for my mothering, I always say it's because I have two rather special daughters to take care of. And my list above only came about because of what you have taught me to hone, and to hold true.

So, Thank You, Rachel and Olivia, for helping me write and rewrite my lists. I hope you each keep a copy of it, to add and take away whenever you shift in life.

I love you, Rachel.

I love you, Olivia. See you at tea-time.

Mama

KAREN TAN has worked with practically every theatre company in Singapore, in a career that has obviously gone on too long. She is the mother of two daughters, nine years apart in age, which marked the points in her life when she needed grounding, good sense, and the true understanding of letting go, and just live.

In Appreciation Of My Daughters

Ng Choong San

My dearest Ysobel and Ericka

When I mentioned that I was planning to write a "thank you" letter to you both, I received a quizzical "Huh?" look from one child, and a curious "Why?" from the other, which in many ways was all for par, but nevertheless also set me thinking.

Have I ever deliberately and intentionally expressed to you my appreciation of you? I know there have been many occasions when your Papa and I have articulated to one another our thankfulness for the pair of you, but I honestly cannot recall if we ever told you the same in your presence. My bad, which I will now attempt—very belatedly—to redress.

Firstly, thank you from the bottom of my heart and soul for putting up with my kaleidoscopic moods. I am reactive, irritable, impatient, blunt, and quick to take offence—often all of these in the space of five minutes and with zero warning. For as long as I can remember, you have faced your mercurial mum with admirable equanimity and when needed, provided comforting words and hugs to soothe ruffled feathers or exhausted psyches. I remember one wet, wintery night in Sydney, I dissolved into tears while complaining about university course mates being unreasonable and irresponsible with group work. You responded by quickly shuffling over on your knees, wiggling into my lap to slide your arms around my neck, and patting my back ever so gently.

This has been repeated with some frequency over the years (at differing intensities), and while I remain clueless as to how you deduced my preference for wordless hugs at such times, I am ever grateful for them! I always worry I must have damaged you in some way by being so unpredictable and emotional. I can only offer unreserved apologies for all the drama, with a promise to do better by you for the future.

Thank you also for your readiness to listen. Lamentations after a hideous day at work, rants and rave during and/or after a drive, stream-of-consciousness musings about the state of the country and society while vegging out in your bedrooms—all have been met with calm, patience, tolerance and validation as well as wit and humour (Me: "XXX is a pain to work with, so ignorant and apathetic!" You: "Oh, he doesn't know and doesn't care?")

And to your everlasting credit, you understand and acknowledge that, nine times out of ten, all I want is a chance to vent in a safe harbour.

Similarly, thank you for being open and honest with me. Confiding how you find it hard to make friends, trying to articulate your mixed feelings about a boy, verbalising your consternation over unfair but accepted social and cultural norms. While our conversations have been contentious and challenging (and often loud), I have always been mightily grateful and relieved that you have felt comfortable enough to share with me as much of your inner selves—thoughts, opinions, perspectives, secrets, fears and everything else in between—as you already have. And I would be over the moon if you would continue to do so for the foreseeable future, and beyond.

I will also try my hardest not to be pushy and intrusive. I have seen how you learn and absorb when you make your own decisions and take ownership of your actions and decisions. Yes, it has been (and will continue to be) painful to see you struggle with projects because of bad time management, or make mistakes in front of an audience because of insufficient practice, but mostly you have emerged with a better understanding of yourself that you apply to make it better the next time around. Having said that, while I am all for independence and self-sufficiency, please also know that there is nothing you cannot tell me that will be a burden I cannot help you bear!

Thank you for being my teachers. From the days you popped into being, my life has been one continuous educational experience with learning curves of all shapes, sizes, and gradients that unobtrusively and unexpectedly permeate other aspects of my life for the better.

From you, I learnt that multi-tasking is over-rated and being in the moment of whatever I am doing is way more productive, case in point being the art and craft projects we did together uninterrupted by household chores and text notifications that turned out better, and more enjoyable, than those churned out in the midst of a mass of other activities.

I've learnt that recognising when to stop and walk away is being smart and not defeatist, such as learning to ignore my maternal instincts and shut the door to wait out Yssey's impossible-to-soothe post-nap crying jags that would magically stop after 10 minutes and leave me with a happy, smiley toddler.

I've learnt that not everything happens for a reason and can be "fixed". Yssey unexpectedly and inexplicably developing asthma in the asthma capital of the world was one such learning moment.

And I hope you never stop calling me out when I'm being judgmental and prejudiced, because my insight can be blinkered and perceptions tainted all too easily toward people and situations I am uncomfortable or unfamiliar with. "How can you make such a generalisation? You don't know XXX!" has become a frequent refrain that pulls me up short

Choong San (centre) with her daughters Ysobel (left) and Ericka (right).

during our conversations. Uncomfortable, to say the least, but admittedly necessary for reflection and staying honest.

Thank you for being my friends. I know mums and daughters who are the tightest of pals that share everything and anything and talk for hours on a daily basis; I also know those whose relationships are so detached or unengaged that "distant" is the kindest way to describe their connection. I think we have found a happy middle-ground: we are not joined at the hip doing everything together, but we keep one another in our thoughts sufficiently to spontaneously send an email, or WhatsApp an emoji to stay connected. Your unexpected texts with attachments of pet-cat and pet-bird antics are an example—totally random but they make me so happy because you send them to your friends, too! And as you have become teenagers, I find myself bouncing ideas off you increasingly frequently because your observations can be as perceptive as those of adults. "Let him think it was his idea, then he'll want to promote it" was a gem you threw me when I grouched about an uncooperative colleague.

Finally, thank you for letting me be me, and loving and trusting this "me"—warts and all—as freely and constantly as you do. I knew motherhood was never going to be a smooth or uncomplicated path to tread, but knowing how you feel about me and the bond we share, I can welcome our future adventures—planned and unplanned—with confidence, courage and hope.

x Mum x

NG CHOONG SAN is an Occupational Therapist who works with persons with dementia at a nursing home. She graduated with a Master in Occupational Therapy from the University of Sydney in 2014, and was employed by various healthcare organisations until her return to Singapore in 2016, where she continued her career at a community hospital.

San also holds a Bachelor of Arts (Honours) in Psychology from the University of Nottingham (1989), and has worked in the military, the arts and healthcare industry. She is married to Shan, a violinist, and they share two teenaged daughters as well as a menagerie of cats, birds and chinchilla. She loves running (when her hips allow), reading biographies and autobiographies (to indulge her inner *kaypoh*), and watching F1 races with her daughters.

When I Was 17

Petrina Kow

Dear Yupi,

When I was 17, I remember walking into school exhausted from the weight and stress of being in "the best institution" and at the same time energised by the buzz of activity moving around in a sea of white and green. This guy ironed his shirt properly. This guy shouldn't wear red underwear. This girl's bra is lacy and black—oooh, risqué. These were the top quality thoughts I was generally pre-occupied with, in addition to who's the cutest guy and which boy was worthy of my attention. You see, coming from an all-girls school, the assumption was that we were "suddenly" exposed to boys and that we were all going to *kee siao* (go nuts) and start whoring ourselves with abandon.

What's the point of this you ask? *Chope.* There's method to the madness. I'm trying very hard to remember what it was really like in school—what kind of person was I and what was I struggling with?—hoping that I'd find some wisdom I could pass down to you.

But here's the truth, I cared not what was happening around the world, or what I wanted to be when I grew up. I cared about who was friends with whom, and what stationery they had. What kind of wisdom could I possibly pass down to you when I am constantly being schooled on how to be a better human by you?

I look at who you are now at 17 and I scan through the fuzzy images of my 17-year-old self back in 1993. And I think, how did I get through all that? When you're surrounded by the messages of "being in the top school" and getting an "elite education", you start believing that you are better than everyone.

Except I didn't feel that way at all. I struggled with that notion of being smart because my grades never quite reflected that. And every year, teachers would write well-meaning comments about "if only she applied herself" or "she should pay attention", or "needs to work harder". Never mind that they always tried to even that out with "has a bubbly personality" or "is friendly and outgoing" or "excellent sportsman"! (That one still makes me laugh)

So I guess I worked hard to be liked. I hung out with smart people hoping it would somehow rub off on me. I marveled at how they seemed to be hanging out in school all day, playing carrom, going to parties and still scoring A's the next day in a test.

I didn't know how to study but I knew how to navigate conversations. I didn't even flinch when teachers would openly insult me in class because I was just so used to it, but I always knew how to be liked. Here's the thing. Knowing how to get people to like you also means that you don't know what you like. You are willing to bend and acquiesce, to not believe in anything because that might change tomorrow depending on what others were saying. It means not standing your ground.

I never quite knew what I wanted, nor had I any resolve to work hard for something because I knew in my gut that was what I wanted. And when I did know what I wanted, people kept telling me that wasn't possible. Don't be an actress. How are you going to make a living? So, I never dared to trust my gut. And soon, I couldn't feel my gut and I didn't know how I felt or what I thought.

I remember that very moment when I handed in my final A Level exam paper. I felt like someone removed a giant rock from my belly I could breathe again. I basically floated out of the room. I remember telling myself, "This is the hardest thing I have ever done!" And then it was as if I never needed to work hard ever again. That is the danger in believing these fallacies you get fed by society. We were trained like sprinters for a bloody ultra marathon. No one ever told me it was okay to fail. There was so much fear and insecurity packed into that moment that you fail to look at what's going on around you. You fail to see how far you've come. You've stopped appreciating all the help you've been given. It's all about you and your achievements. Once again. But *it's not*.

This idea of pass or fail is so baked into our psyche as Singaporeans that it's tempting to fall into an easy binary. There are no opposites. Things are never just pass or fail, good or bad, right or wrong. Everything we do is a process. We may not always know what we are doing or why, but sitting with it and facing it is the bravest thing we can do. Becoming intimate with the process of fear and uncertainty allows you to dismantle the familiar ways of being.

I love this quote from *When Things Fall Apart* by Tibetan Buddhist nun and teacher, Pema Chödrön:

> "Things falling apart is a kind of testing and also a kind of healing. We think that the point is to pass the test or to overcome the problem, but the truth is that things don't really get solved. They come together and they fall apart. Then they come together again and fall apart again. It's just like that. The healing comes from letting there be room for all of this to happen: room for grief, for relief, for misery, for joy."

I remember when you burst into my world. I was barely formed myself, still reeling from the knowledge that my own mother might be dying. I suddenly found myself holding a life. You. I had no idea what I was doing. I had no friends around me who'd lived through it that I could talk to. I felt very alone. Yet, for some reason I had a stiff spine. I felt like whatever happened, I had to suck it up and appear to everyone that I had it all under control. I couldn't bend, I couldn't take a break. I had to work and do something all the time. My gut. I couldn't feel it. I cried all the time. Sometimes at nothing. I had no idea what I was crying about or why and the smallest things triggered me. When I couldn't soothe you, I envisioned thoughts of throwing you out the window. I didn't know what was wrong with me. Yet like everything else I'd learnt in life up to that point, I would fold it all up and shove it down deep in my gut until I didn't know it was there. It all sounds terribly dark and morbid, but there was also so much joy amidst the grief and pain. You were a much needed light in my life especially when I knew my mother didn't have much longer. You made everyone happy. You were the first grandchild for Nai Nai and Ye Ye—they were overjoyed and would find any excuse to spoil you. And they still do!

I remember once when we were visiting my mother, your Por Por, she was lying in bed not moving very much with a tube down her nose to help her breathe. You were only two years old but you knew. You always had an ability to sense a room. You felt people's energy and knew instinctively what they needed before they did. I saw you go up to her bedside, and reach for her hand. And when the prayer group came along to sing some hymns, you came to me and told me to ask them to leave because Por Por was sleeping and needed rest. You were two! You also spoke in full sentences and properly enunciated EVERYTHING. But I digress.

You were an inquisitive and all-sensing child. Almost sentient. Like you had come implanted with wisdom from the ancients. In large noisy playgroups you would sit along the sidelines to observe and take in the room. I would instinctively push you to interact, but after a while, I knew you had your own mind and your own timeline. Nobody could get you to do anything you didn't want to do. When it came time for school, the struggles we had! Haha! It's almost hilarious thinking about it now. Remember the time I battled with you to do colouring homework? I mean, which seven-year-old kid doesn't want to colour? You didn't see the point. So after reasoning with you for a good two hours, I coloured your damn homework. You were always all in or nothing.

I remember the phases you had. When you were two or three, you would be taken by a book and we would have to read that book over and over. And even when I suggested others, you would make me read it again and again. In fact, you had memorised all of it, making me think you were a child genius and could read at such an early age!

At seven years old, you devoured collections of fairy books, then it was Greek mythology then it was Percy Jackson, James Patterson, Harry Potter, then Brandon Sanderson. Then when you hit secondary school, it was K-pop then anime and now, all things Japanese. You were reading manga in Chinese even! Haha! A true *Otaku*. I am genuinely bemused because I was just so different at your age. I think you read more books in the first seven years of your life than I have in my entire life!

The first three years of your secondary school life were tough, innit? Unlike me, you had no troubles with your academic work. But like me, you were very concerned with how others perceived you. I guess that's what they call being a teenager? I remember these struggles clearly as it wasn't so long ago. I was worried. You weren't sleeping well, you were allergic to everything. Changes in temperature, when it was too cold, too hot. Light too bright. Your stress was manifesting in your skin and gut. Stomachaches. Headaches. Pain. The doctor visits, the calls from school. I didn't know how to deal with it and again I stiffened my back and went to work. Things were falling apart, but with time and some gathered wisdom, we crawled, sat, struggled, and got back up again. I always took my cue from you. Again, you taught me that. I learnt how to approach you not to "fix" or "cure" or "solve", but to just sit and be. To just listen and hold. Man, it was hard. From a lifetime of shoving and swallowing and stiffening and working, to just sit and listen and hold and soothe. You developed language for me so I knew when you needed my intervention, or just shut up and listen. I am still learning.

I remember that very moment in my certification class when my voice teacher Catherine Fitzmaurice said "all research is me-search'. There are days I have so much I want to share. I want to tell you to read this article, understand these concepts, learn meditation, have a physical practice. This will help with that. Then I realise, I am trying to fix. Then I breathe, and I remember my gut. In fact, I am feeling my gut now. It's big, a little gassy if I'm being honest. It's soft and flabby. It's held two humans. I have stretch marks. I wouldn't mind if it was a little flatter but these days, I rub my "softy belly" and remember what a gift it bore.

Journeying with you has been the most satisfying and graceful thing I've done in my life. I have so much fear and anxiety about your future. I want to protect you from all possible forms of shit that might come your way. I don't want you to hurt. But I know that's part of learning and healing. You know, it's been 15 years since my mother passed away. We talk a lot about Por Por. I make sure to tell you her stories. She was a formidable woman. She was flawed like all of us, but she fought with everything she had. She made things with her hands. She sculpted, weaved, moulded and fired. She did this with her students and her art. She

Petrina (left) and her daughter Yupi.

taught me to live a life for others whilst always in pursuit of bettering oneself. She didn't have to tell me anything. She did it by living her life, and I see it in the lives she's touched. I still think a lot about her. I miss her and I wonder if she's proud of me. It's so funny because she's dead and I'm still trying to seek her approval. I touch my belly and I remind myself of the connection we have. I don't need her approval. I know she's proud of me. You know why? Because I look at you and I realise how much I love you and how proud I am of you. Not because you've done anything or not done anything. There is nothing to do.

I have said I don't always know many things and I'm just learning to listen and trust my gut again. But I know this: you will be fine. I want you to walk this world with your head held high with confidence and knowledge that you are whole and beautiful and loved. It is not dependent on what you do and who you love and what you decide to be. You don't have to do a damn thing to be loved. You just are.

PETRINA KOW is the first and only Certified Fitzmaurice Voicework® teacher based in Singapore. She is the founder of Vocal Presence Pte Ltd and teaches Voice and Accents at LaSalle College of the Arts and Nanyang Academy of Fine Art. She conducts workshops and leads corporate groups in storytelling, voice and presentation. She is also a highly sought-after voice actor, an ex-radio deejay, and emcee/host for corporate and family events. She is one of the founders of Telling Stories Live, a live storytelling event that hopes to build empathy through the courageous act of sharing personal stories.

Lessons My Four Daughters Taught Me

Dawn Sim

To my daughters Nyx, Nya, Nyla and Nykki,

Bringing up the four of you has been and still is my greatest source of joy and lessons in life. As much as I've strived to best teach you what you need to know in life, I must say that I'm truly grateful to also be on the receiving end of what being a mother to you girls has taught me.

My journey as a mother to you girls really began when I was just 26 years old and had left my job in Singapore to be with your father in France for four years. This was where Nyx and Nya were both born and raised for the first few years of your lives. I always thought that being an active person would mean I would have an easy delivery, so I didn't expect that I would end up having to go through emergency Caesarean sections with the two of you after many hours of labour. Now I know that your level of fitness does not determine whether or not you will have an easy delivery, but I sure am grateful that I've always been an active person, even throughout my pregnancies. That made it so much easier for me to recover from the major abdominal surgery. Being active was also what made my post-natal days more bearable, since it helped me have the strength and stamina to do what I needed to do as mom, breastfeeding and taking care of the household when your Dad went back to work. So my darlings, please remember this when it is your turn to be a mom. You need to make sure that you continue your exercise when you're pregnant, so that your early days as a mother will be so much easier.

Each one of you gave me such a different experience during pregnancy and you all have such different personalities which makes my life truly a colourful and exciting one.

Nyx, I remember how I often cried myself to sleep when I was spotting during my first trimester—I was so worried that you were in danger.

Nya, I cried buckets every single day at the hospital in Southern France where you were born—you had to be treated for jaundice, and I had to watch you stay under the UV lights and throw up your milk a few times.

Nyla, the first two weeks of your life was spent in and out of the hospital; syringes entering your arms, spinal fluid drawn from you at a few days old, daily trips to the hospital to go on the drip. All this when your Dad had to leave for a mission five days after you were born—and he didn't see you again till you were five weeks old.

Nykki, with you, I had so much difficulty walking and moving the in my last month of my pregnancy. A few months after giving birth, I had pubic symphysis which caused excruciating pain to my pelvis. But despite all these emotionally and physically painful experiences, I would do it all over again to have the four of you in my life.

Nyx, you have always been such a great help to me from the time you were a toddler. When Nya was born you immediately had that sisterly love for her and would always run to help me in caring for her. From fetching the diapers and wet wipes to helping me hold her bottle for her, you were always there to help, and you still help Mommy in so many ways to this day. Thank you. Your nurturing nature reminds me of how I teach you to care for others and to always be kind, and I love that you teach your sisters that too.

Nya, your resourcefulness and love for exploration makes you such a wild child among your sisters—there's never a dull moment when you're around. Thank you for using your resourcefulness and ability to solve problems quickly to help your sisters learn and understand things. Keep experimenting and discovering all there is to learn, and keep your life exciting, my darling.

Nyla, your honesty and sincerity has brought you valuable friendships even from those as old as your grandfather. I remember being so surprised when you walked up to a stall owner at the hawker centre and explained to him the harm of smoking. You were only three. By the time you turned eight, we had attended the weddings of the children of these stall owners who have now become our friends who gave up smoking because of you. Your sincerity truly is something that Mommy looks up to.

Nykki, you have the advantage of learning so much from your three older sisters. Which is why you tend to behave older than your four years of age now. I love that you have no fear of finding out how things work and why things are the way they are. Your attention to detail sometimes baffles me, especially when you know exactly where things are in the house. I can't wait to see how you will continue to surprise me as you develop and mature.

Girls, you are all so different even though Mommy and Daddy brought you all up the same way and love you all the same. But know that even though you are different, that bond and that love that you have for each other will keep you together. And you will need to hold one another's hands, in the same way that my sister, your *Yiyi* (aunt), and I still do. You may argue and you may disagree sometimes, but that will always pass. Family and the love we have for one another should never be taken for granted.

The past three years that your dad had an overseas posting in the USA was an incredibly challenging period for me, having to take care of the four of you while setting up a new fitness studio and running the business. So many times I asked myself if I was shortchanging you girls by teaching and managing a business at the same time.

But looking back on all this right now, I wouldn't change a thing. The precious lessons and skills that I've learnt and refined have made me an even better version of myself as a mother and an individual. More importantly I know that you have also learnt so much from me through these experiences: you've seen how I prioritize my time and make my decisions so that you know that you are the most important to me.

You always knew that the weekends would be family fun time for us even though I had to play mommy and daddy while your dad was away. And that meant making sure that

I got my work and commitments done so that we could be present for one another. I want to thank you girls for being so understanding and hearing me out whenever we needed to talk through things and the times I had to discipline you. Communication and straight talk between us is really the key to making things work, and I am grateful for the fact that we started early on this together. Remember this not just when you become mothers yourselves, but with people whom you care about and work with. Trust is built on these two things, and without them, things just fall apart.

Even though we only saw your Dad two or three times a year during the three years he was away, the time that we got to spend together will stay etched in our hearts and memories because we always made it a point to be present with one another. Thank you for understanding when mommy restricted the use of mobile devices.

My decision to wake up before 6am every day to do my work and to get my exercise done was so that I could be more present with you girls when you were awake and we could do things together without me worrying about my to-do list.

You should also know that the consistent exercise has always been a priority for me because it helps me be a better a mother. Without it my energy levels and mood take a nose dive and I just feel like I'm not giving you my best. I hope that the encouragement and habits that I impart to you now to exercise every day will stay with you even throughout your adulthood and you will continue to look after yourselves the same way I'm showing you now—if not in better ways.

Remember that nobody can help you do the exercise that your body needs but yourselves, and you already know what a difference it makes to the quality of your day especially when you get it done in the mornings. I do so look forward to us being able to continue having fun in my senior years with you girls and my grandchildren!

So many times over the past few years when I've had to bring you girls along with me to work, you've always only shown me patience and understanding and I couldn't be more thankful for that. Not once have I heard a complaint or disgruntled remark, and I always ask myself what I did to make this magic happen. I believe it has to be the way that we talk and listen to one another, and I hope that you will continue to do so for your friends and other people whom you care about.

Many times, I whisper a thank you under my breath when I hear you all take turns to invite your parents, grandparetns and senior to "*Jiak*!" (eat) at meal times. This is a family tradition and my wish is that you will teach your children the same respect for their elders.

So many times I shed a tear when I find your love notes to me stuffed into my bag when I'm out and about working during the day.

My darlings, you have no idea how much energy and encouragement I get from you each and every day—they help me work through my challenges and difficult times as a mother and a business owner. Often we may fall into the trap of centering our thoughts on the negative—that's toxic and dangerous as it will affect your mindset, and your entire outlook. We always have a choice, my babies—I want you to always remember that. You can choose to see the same situation in a positive or a negative way, but it will affect your decisions and how well you respond to others. I know that I make a conscious choice to stay positive despite being in challenging situations, and it has always helped to make my days better, especially when I know that I do not want negativity to affect the way I communicate with the ones I care about the most: you girls.

I hope that this letter is something that you will read again and again, my darlings, because what I say to you now may not ring a bell till some other lessons have been learnt and some other experiences have been gained. But one thing I hope you will never forget is gratitude. We all have people to be grateful for. I could never get where I am without the support and encouragement of your grandparents and of course, your father and my sister throughout my journey. Family is where it all begins, and I want for you girls to be there for one another through this journey that is life. Hold hands and support one another through the tough times and celebrate successes together. Know that life is filled with ups and downs and challenges, but the right mindset and grit will help make this journey a whole lot more enjoyable and meaningful.

I love you more than you will ever know.

Mommy

Entrepreneur and owner of Trium Fitness, now in its fourth year, **DAWN SIM** has always had a passion for fitness and sports and has been teaching yoga and Pilates for over 19

Dawn Sim (centre) with her four daughters.

years. As a hands-on parent who prefers teaching her children, aged 4 through 14, through experiential learning, she values interaction and communication with her children—that bond makes it easier for her to understand them. Although she handles running a business, teaching and looking after her family, Dawn also values the importance of looking after herself and sets aside time every day to achieve that.

My Motherhood Experiment

Chiong Xiao Ting

Dear Jaime,

Fortunately (or unfortunately), you are my firstborn. When I was pregnant with you, I was 26 and I gave birth to you at 27. By our society's standard, I would be considered a young mum, but definitely not so in my mother's times.

The huge difficulty I faced being a first-time mum was that I grew up mostly without a mother. My Dad and Mum were separated not long after I was born, and Mum had to raise me all by herself. She had to work hard to provide for the family and take care of me. For most part of my childhood, we were in survival mode.

I remember how she would take up multiple jobs, and it seemed like she tried everything possible, from selling property, to tutoring, to clerical work—she even resorted to being a part-time cleaner to earn extra bucks. I did not find anything abnormal with that lifestyle—I would follow her everywhere she went, whether it was to her tutee's home, or to the houses she had to clean on the weekends. This was the norm I embraced and enjoyed.

My aunties and our family friends would often tell me how my Mum struggled to take care of me when I was small. How sickly I was, how difficult it was to find a babysitter for me, how helpless Mum was. But all this didn't mean much to me until I became a mother. In my head, I had understood that it was difficult, but it was only when I became a mum could I empathise with what she had gone through, and learnt to truly appreciate all that she had done for me.

The year I turned eight, Mum discovered some health issues during her routine medical check-up. A few months later, I was told that she had cancer. In those days, cancer wasn't as common as it is now. Truth be told, a 9-year-old at that time would not know anything about cancer. I only knew that Mum was sick—quite sick, in fact—and that she might not be able to take care of me.

I had to move to my Uncle's to be under the care of my Aunty. In the months that followed, I saw how cancer robbed Mum of her life bit by bit, until I lost her completely. Mum was a very strong, independent woman, but she slowly shrivelled away because of the sickness and chemotherapy. I remember that in the last months before her passing, I dreaded visiting her because she was no longer the Mum I knew, and I really did not know how to process the emotions and deal with all these that was coming my way.

When I was 10, I lost my mum to cancer.

To say that it was devastating would probably be an understatement, but growing with Mum all these years, I had learnt only one way to deal with things: to be strong. When faced with life's difficulties, my Mum had only one mode of operation, and that was to be strong and to survive. Hence, since I was young, this was the only way I know how to deal with things: to be strong and to survive.

Mum never spoke to me about her cancer, her sickness, her pain—anything she faced. Before she passed on, she had put everything in place, instructed various people to carry out what she wanted, made sure that I would be well taken care of. But I don't remember her saying any last words to me. That was my Mum—she would not reveal her weaker side, or express her pain and grief. In a sense, that was how I learnt to deal with my emotions.

I recall going back to school the next day after the funeral was over, and my teacher had told the class that my mother had just passed away. One of my classmates turned and said to me very innocently, "You don't look like your mum had just died." I did not know how to respond, nor did I cry and become emotional. I did not know how I was supposed to "look like". This was the survival mechanism I had inherited from Mum: that in the most difficult circumstances, you can be strong and just forge on.

In my growing up years, even with the absence of a mother, I did forge on. After Mum's passing, I studied hard and worked hard, scoring A's, making my way to top schools and I guess, I did Mum proud.

Many years later, I became a mother myself. Your Daddy and I did not have much help, and though I had my in-laws, it was different not having your own mother walking through this journey with you. Being strong and independent by nature, I did not ask for help and managed most things on my own, with your Daddy's help, of course.

But Daddy was often busy at work, so most of the time it was just you and me. I loved those moments alone with you; it was great bonding time and it often reminded me of those days that I had with Mum, just following her from place to place. That was what I did with you too—you simply went with me from place to place, and wherever I went, you would follow.

I had high hopes to "train" you, the way my Mum did me, to become this strong and independent young lady. But alas, your personality is quite the opposite. You are very sensitive, persistent and you have a strong personality. As a young child, you were very sticky and, somehow, insecure. You would cry whenever we stepped into an unfamiliar house. You would break down when strangers talked to you, and by strangers, I mean anybody other than Daddy or Mummy!

Where was that strong, independent girl that I had envisioned? Many times, I would get sympathetic or disapproving looks (depending on the observer's parenting philosophy), or the elders in the family would make well-meaning comments that ended up annoying me. You were not a typical baby that enjoyed others' attention—you only wanted Mummy. When we were home, you could not play independently and I had to be by your side almost all the time.

But I was determined to train you, and like how I was "ruthless" with myself, I was pretty "ruthless" with you. I had no qualms about allowing you to have meltdowns—I would not adhere to your requests because I felt that that was spoiling you. During your meltdowns, you would want nothing but Mummy, and I would walk out of the room just to leave you alone to "grow up" and "get your act together".

Yet, in recent years, I have started to question myself: have I forced you to grow up too fast? Have I not given you the space and security you need to develop emotionally? Have I failed to recognise that you are different? And most importantly, have I imposed the very same survival mode that I had inherited from my Mum on you?

You turned 7 this year, and there are days that I am still dealing with your meltdowns. Sometimes it is unbelievable to me that you still have these moments. During these times, it seems like you are regressing back to toddlerhood, and I start reflecting that I should have held you longer, calmed you further, and not force you to grow up prematurely. Yes, I am learning, baby. These moments sometimes frustrate me greatly, but I am pushing myself to hold you longer, to tell you it is okay, that Mummy is here, though as I'm doing it, my mind is saying you should grow up and stop behaving like this. But, Jaime, we are in this together!

Turning 7 is a huge milestone because it means that you now enter into formal education: primary school. Education is a big deal for us in Singapore, hence many parents do their utmost to secure a place for their children in the best school possible. I was blessed because my Mum recognised the importance of education, and she managed to secure a place for me in a SAP (special assistance plan) school—it's a place for academically bright students who are strong in both English and their mother tongue. I loved my alma mater; this school held precious memories for me, and it was the place that I had excelled and thrived in in the most difficult season in my life— when Mum passed away. I was determined to send you there too, even though it meant that you had to be on the school bus an hour in the morning and another hour home. But I was hopeful that you would replicate the success I had academically.

Being an alumna, I registered you for the school with no hiccups at all. I was elated. However, there was a nagging feeling on the inside of me that I could not shake. Numerous promptings from God made me rethink my decision. Doubts and questions began to surface: in this time and era, do I really need to send my daughter to a "branded school" so that she can maybe gain a head-start in life? I was challenged in all areas: What do I value more? Do I value your happiness in your childhood years over your academic success? Do I need to put you through two hours on the bus daily just so that you can attend a seemingly better school?

I battled with all these thoughts for many days, only to relent to God's leading at the last minute. I deregistered you from my alma mater, and signed you up for the "neighbourhood school" next to our home.

I wept over this decision for days. I felt a deep sense of loss that you would probably not walk in my footsteps and replicate my success. In those moments, I recognised that I needed to let go and allow you to live the life that God has created you for. You are you, and I am me. I cannot—and must not—impose my dreams on you, and I must allow you to discover all the gifts God has placed in you.

These days, there is a simple joy in my heart, when I see how happy you are to wake up each morning for school. You don't struggle with the early mornings, you look forward to school and you enjoy your classes so much every single day. I have come to realise that this is the most important thing: your happiness and well-being.

You have come a long way from that insecure baby who would only cling to me and no one else. These days, you are expressive and confident. You have taken on primary school like a champ: you fiercely pursue and persevere at the things you take interest in. You love tagging along wherever I go, to the office, for work assignments, to run errands. Not so long ago, you even followed me on a work-cum-leisure trip overseas. To be honest, I genuinely enjoy bringing you places, and you have become the strong and independent lady I hoped for, and more.

Thank you for being my firstborn. I knowingly (or unknowingly) put greater pressure on you as you are the big sister. I am often more demanding of you because you are the older one. But you have taken on all these responsibilities so well. You have grown up to be a great older sister to your *Meimei* (younger sister). You would give in to her or try to

Chiong Xiao Ting and her daughter Jaime.

navigate your way around things, even when she is at times demanding. I am so proud to see how you are growing, not just intellectually, but also emotionally, socially, physically and spiritually.

Thank you, Jaime, for allowing me to "experiment" motherhood on you. I am learning and you are too, and we have both come a long way. I am glad that every new day is a day for me to become a better mother, to undo the mistakes of my past, and to help you become all that God wants you to be. In these seven short years, you have taught me so much, and helped me become a much better version of myself. You will always have a special place in my heart and I can't wait to see how you will blossom in the future to come.

Love you so much,
Mummy

CHIONG XIAO TING is a millennial mum with two daughters, seven and four. Having come from a difficult family background, she often has her own unique perspective and take on life—she believes in taking the road less travelled. Upon graduation from Nanyang Technological University with a Bachelor's Degree in Chinese, Xiao Ting went on to become a Mandarin translator for her church—her first and only job ever since. She hopes to impart her passion for life, for her faith and her love for Chinese to her children. Her greatest desire is that they live the fullest lives possible, and believe that the sky is the limit for them.

Part 2

WHEN LIFE THROWS YOU LEMONS

"Having children just puts the whole world into perspective. Everything else just disappears."
—Kate Winslet

The Incredible Story Of Why We Moved To New Zealand

Adlena Wong

Dear Keri and Ava

When Mummy was asked to write a letter to you two as part of a book of letter from mothers to their daughters, I was stunned. Stunned not only because it has been a long while since Mummy wrote anything decent—much less a 3,000-word essay, but also how could I, an inexperienced mother to two young girls compare with other accomplished mothers? What could I share that other mothers don't already know or haven't been through. But that's your mother for you.

For as long as I can remember, I have always had these high internal standards. I don't know where this came from or how these benchmarks came about. I'm guessing it has in part to do with being the first granddaughter and the first daughter of a military father.

Being the first meant that I was constantly used as a yardstick, the standard to which my younger sibling and cousins had to live up to. This also meant that I grew up in a home where spontaneity was almost non-existent, disrespect was punishable and self-reliance and discipline were expected.

For the most part of my life, holding myself to these high standards has been a good thing.

What these high standards meant was that when Mummy was not doing great at math, I would buy assessment books with pocket money that I had earned from tutoring younger kids. And I sought out tutors to help me improve at math.

It meant that, as a school runner, when I needed to shave seconds off my 800-metre timing, I would ask for extra training, even if it meant missing recess, or having to train twice a day, three times a week during the school holidays.

It meant that, to get that A in General Paper, I would write one essay a day and shove it in my teacher's pigeon hole daily, to the point she told me to stop because she hadn't finished marking my previous papers.

Mummy got that A, by the way. Did better than most Arts students in math (and was even asked by my math teacher if I wanted to join the 'S' paper group). And I can claim that 2 minutes 39 seconds is my best timing for two rounds around the track.

But as I grew older, and especially when I had you, Keri, I started to realise that wanting to be perfect, responsible and consistent all the time can work against a person. Instead of making you feel good because you're always seeking to make things better for yourself and others, it can make you feel alone, like you're the only one with the standards and expectations, and disappointed, unappreciated and worse of all, hypercritical of yourself. You wind up feeling like it's impossible to catch a break.

The quest to be good, right and balanced is tiring.

Mummy felt it the most when you were born Keri. And I felt it for days, months and years after.

Like Mummy, you were the first grandchild—at least on the side of the family that "mattered". What that meant was everyone wanted a piece of you. And everyone had an opinion of how you needed to be fed, carried, taught and raised, based on how they were fed, carried, taught and raised. That didn't sit well with me and caused a lot of tension between your Daddy, his family and I. Mummy genuinely thought that my marriage wouldn't survive your fourth birthday, Keri.

But given the history of damaging relationships, failed marriages and poor accountability from the people who mattered most to me growing up, the thought of history repeating itself scared me more than having to contend with difficult in-laws and your Daddy, whom Mummy found out along the way is a man who, while generous, thoughtful and forgiving is also one who needs reminding and reassuring.

Mummy has been reading books and listening to podcasts on mental health, how to deal with trauma and somatic theory, things like that. All that only convinces me that whatever negative experiences or distress I have lived through, the buck stops with me.

At this point, you may both be wondering, "What happened that made you this way, Mummy?"

It probably started with my first memory of being hauled, together with your *Yiyi* (then barely two years old), into the back seat of my father's—your Ah Gong—car and driven around looking for my mother, your Nenek, who had run away from home. For what reason, Mummy never found out.

I remember we even drove across the Causeway to Moyang's (Mummy's maternal grandmother) searching for her, only to be told Nenek wasn't there. I don't recall what happened after that. I just remember the day my mother returned home to us.

It took Mummy some years to connect the dots but it turned out Nenek was not a happily married woman. Nenek and Ah Gong argued often—over what exactly, I wasn't sure. Sometimes they would go for days not talking or acknowledging each other. I guess the fact that Ah Gong was often away on overseas military exercises and Nenek worked 12-hour night shifts in factory assembly lines made things more tolerable between them. Maybe it served to delay the inevitable.

Some relatives speculated that their marriage wasn't working out because of the background and cultural differences between them. After all, Nenek was a Javanese-Malay girl from a poor family in a small kampong in Malaysia, while Ah Gong had a strict and traditional Chinese father who was adamant his son shouldn't have to convert to Islam nor take on a Muslim name and identity. However, that issue was apparently smoothened out when I came into the picture—peace on condition that I would be recognised as Chinese, studied Chinese in school, and took on a Chinese name, which explains why Mummy doesn't have a "Binte" in my name, like most Muslim-born children do.

Other people speculated that difficulties arose because it was an arranged marriage between my parents. Nenek was introduced to Ah Gong by her older sister—Ah Gong was the nephew of her sister's husband. Word had it that it was a marriage Nenek entered into reluctantly.

Mummy can only imagine the pressure Nenek must have felt. First, she had an older sister assuring her Ah Gong was the right choice. In addition, Nenek's father was also proud and comforted by the idea that his daughter would be marrying into a Chinese family in Singapore—a move that meant an "upgrade" and an opportunity for a better life.

Why Mummy is sharing all this with you is because, not only do I find an uncanny resemblance between what Nenek went through in her marriage and what I've gone through in mine, but also, I wish to prepare you for when your turn comes.

The thing is, when you are the "minority"—in Nenek's and Mummy's case, Muslim women marrying into traditional Chinese families—you need to be prepared to be scrutinised, questioned and to work doubly, triply hard to prove your worth and standing in the family who took you in.

When you are different and foreign, people fear you and categorise you as "other" because they can't figure you out and they don't really know what to do with you. I remember, days before Daddy was due to convert to Islam, your father's mother, your *Nai Nai* asked, to my chagrin, "Do I have to call him Mohammed from now on?"

It is no coincidence Mummy is writing this against the backdrop of the Black Lives Matter movement going on all over the world right now. Coupled with the realisation that in 20 years or so, both of you are likely to be marrying a Kiwi, I promise you, even in 2045, you are going to be asked pointed questions about your race, background, culture, heritage. You'll be put in difficult positions by the ignorant, the bigoted and the out-of-touch.

Certain conversations are difficult to be had. Have them anyway. Don't be like Mummy, Keri and Ava. Remember what Dr Seuss said? "Be who you are and say what you feel, because those who mind don't matter and those who matter don't mind."

Be braver than Mummy ever was and speak up when you're called upon and not suffer in silence just because you are not in the "majority", "position" or "colour" to do so. I have been so eager to please and to keep the peace that I have, on too many occasions, dumbed down my answers and stifled my honest feelings. Unfortunately for me, Nenek isn't the kind of mother who is good with articulating her feelings—she's not someone I can have heart-to-heart talks with. I promise I will do this differently with you girls, because the buck stops with me.

As a matter of fact, there are a few other things I want to do differently from what I was shown, taught and told.

The first thing—if you haven't already noticed—is to bring you up in an environment that's totally different from what Mummy grew up in. New Zealand was an accidental find. I did fall in love with it when I first visited in 2013, not aware I was pregnant with you then, Keri. The subsequent two times we came here with you kind of sealed the deal: the space, the crisp air, the quiet it is full of, the absence of the senseless mad rush of Singapore. The truth is—the time is nigh that Mummy comes clean now—that apart from Singapore, there was also something else I was annoyed with and wanted to get far, far away from.

My family.

I have always felt like one of the unlucky few to grow up in a family that makes me feel I am never enough; that, when bad things happen, it's always my fault. I thought that if I tried to be good (read: become the prefect, class monitor, captain of track and field team) and do good (read: be in the top three in class from primary 1 to 3, top 10 per cent in the O Level graduating class), my family would perhaps show up once in a while to watch me race, or at least, not mess up and stay together. But that was not meant to be for me.

As if having to contend with parents in an unhappy marriage my whole life was not enough to break me, Mummy had to find out, in the most traumatic way possible, that my father is gay.

Of course, the person who hurt the most was Nenek. As a wife and a mother myself now, I can only imagine how she must have felt. At that time, it was so inconceivable that it took several attempts, and seeing it with my own eyes, to be convinced that my family would never be the same again.

When I told this to my grandmother, my aunties and uncles, no one believed me—they called me a liar. I had to show them text messages (Ah Gong was quite a careless person) inadvertently left in the phone that was handed down to me.

Now, don't get Mummy wrong. Ah Gong coming out was not what I had an issue with. It was how he dealt with the repercussions. Finding out in the way that she did dealt a huge blow to Nenek: she tried to jump off a building. I didn't know whether it was Ah Gong who managed to convinced her not to, or she was overcome by her faith. Either way, I am grateful that Nenek didn't go through with it.

Discovering all of this and still having to live under one roof (because Nenek and I couldn't afford to move out on our own at the time) meant having to swallow our pride.

That's why when Daddy and I got married and bought our first house, I was so happy and relieved because I no longer was under Ah Gong's mercy. But little did I know that my father had other plans. Instead of fulfilling his end of the bargain after their divorce to buy Nenek a place, Ah Gong said to me, "Since you have your own place now, your mother should live with you because it's your responsibility to take care of her." He had defrauded his own mother, your great-grandmother of her home when his father died, and now he was doing it again, this time to his wife who had stuck by him for more than 20 years.

That was what I could not forgive him for.

For years, this was a thorn in Mummy's flesh. There was always some mess caused by someone in the family that Mummy had to clean up. I was tired of this.

The one-way ticket to New Zealand took Mummy years to plan. Mummy has Daddy to thank for that. No doubt it took some cajoling and wrestling, because why would Daddy, who was so comfortable all his life, whose career was taking off in Singapore, want to give all of that up and start all over again in a foreign land?

The second thing I want to do differently, and I hope you do too, is, once in a while, do something that scares you. Growing up in Singapore, we are conditioned to be afraid of what's out there. The common refrain we heard before moving was, "Singapore is so good, clean, safe. Why do you want to leave?" Well, let me tell you something, girls, Mummy didn't get this far in life by being scared into submission. So, I may be nervous about bungy jumping, and I may not have tattoos inked all over, but Mummy is bad ass that way. The truest and best form of badassery comes from within—you only show your hand when the time is right. That's probably the best advice Mummy can give you. Was it scary to leave my birth country, where I had spent my entire life? Sure.

Was it scary to do that with two young children in tow? Of course.

Was it scary to do that with no job waiting for either of us on the other side? That goes without saying.

Was it scary to do that with a finite amount of life savings? Certainly.

Was it scary to know that after all that we have put into this, we may fail and have to go back to where we came from? Hell to the yes.

It was frightening for both Mummy and Daddy but Daddy did it for me, and Mummy did it for me, and I'm doing it for you both. Because I know I cannot heal in the environment that made me sick and when I'm not healed, I will hurt you and that's the last thing I want. Because remember, the buck stops with me.

Maybe it's the physical distancing—being 8,000 km away from your pain helps—but Mummy hasn't felt so free, so unjudged, so unriddled with other people's responsibilities, so unworried about the Joneses, for a very long time. And because I'm not shackled, I can finally work on my dream: to own and run a food truck!

If only I had known earlier that all the paths I'd taken would lead me to a food truck business in New Zealand, I wouldn't have spent all those crazy hours memorising history facts or plowed all that money into math tuition. I'm kidding—you still need to study, okay?

Mummy didn't have much career luck: the magazine I loved working at closed down prematurely. I had some really sucky bosses who cared more about their KPIs than nurturing me. I just wasn't at the right place at the right time most times. I would have loved to stay in a company for 10 years too like everybody else, you know.

Yet, as corny as it sounds, Mummy always believes that things happen for a reason.

My life and work experiences—my days as a barista at Coffee Bean & Tea Leaf, a horror-story writer, a server at hotel banquets—are all coming together to give Mummy everything I need at this point in my life: to be a mom, to be a wife, to adjust to living in a new country and to run a food business.

Ultimately, what Mummy hopes to share with you, Keri and Ava, are these 10 things:

- Whatever experience you have—good and bad—embrace it with the knowledge that someday, somehow it will be of use even though everything in the universe may be telling you otherwise at that point in time. Because, as Mummy's favourite monk, Ajahn Brahm, likes to say, "Good, bad, who knows?"

- Speak up. Even when it's inconvenient. But especially when it's inconvenient.

- Try. Some people are good at one thing, others at many things. It doesn't matter which group you belong to as long as you remember it takes trying to be good at just one thing, or many things. So, for good or for bad, try your darndest.

- Care for and help others, especially those who don't ask for it, because more often than not, they're the ones who need it the most.

Adlena with her daughters Keri and Ava.

- Do the right thing even when no one's looking. When no one's looking, just keep doing your thing—one day, someone *will* see it.
- Always start with trust and respect for others. Unless they do something to lose your trust or disrespect you, then you tell them they have to earn it.
- Mummy makes mistakes and doesn't have all the answers. I learn from you as much as you learn from me. Let's be kind to each other and grow together.
- Don't waste your time and energy on people who don't matter or who make you feel unworthy. I hope you will learn sooner than later that doing things to please people will only make you miserable.
- Don't give up so easily. Good things are worth the struggle. Learn something because it interests you, benefits you and grows you. Don't learn just to score good grades.
- Girls are strong, powerful, brave, and we can do anything that we set our hearts and minds to. Don't let anyone— especially boys—tell you otherwise.

Mummy remembers this so clearly. Once I was asked by a friend, "Why do you want to have kids?" My reply was, "Because I'm curious how they will turn out."

You know what, six years into it now, I very much am. I'm sure 60 years later, I will still say the same thing.

Mummy loves you girls so much. No matter what happens, where you are, how you do, I will always be proud of you.

ADLENA WONG is a third-generation Singaporean born of Straits-born Chinese, Malay and Javanese heritage. She was told when she's born, her jaundice was so severe that she had to have a blood transfusion— which may explain a little why she's an apple that's fallen pretty far from the proverbial tree. After many hard conversations with her husband, life savings emptied out, fretting and worrying and countless moves, Adlena now finds herself with her two young children in tow in the Land of the Long White Cloud, determined to prove that there is more to life than getting good grades and mindless busy-ness. She also gets to fulfil her long-time dream of cooking and serving food out of a food truck.

Triumphing Over Life's Challenges

Kalthum Ahmad

To my three dearest, beloved daughters,

Now that I have seen you all grown-up, bloomed and blossomed, each having chosen the right man for a husband, bringing up children of your own in the right path and direction, being good mothers to them—my most important duties are accomplished, and I am full of love and admiration for you. You have continued the values Daddy and I have imparted to you, through guiding you since you were born.

It's time now to pen and share my life story with you.

Growing up, I always had people around me. I lived with my grandmother in a family bungalow with unmarried aunties and three uncles. The house was full of life and laughter; it was noisy but joyful. We learnt to respect each other, especially the elders. Family guests were frequent—they would be there either for meals or tea. My grandmother was a warm person. She ensured that there was food for all guests. She taught me that sharing food will bring many blessings and will not make you any poorer.

My late grandmother was my best friend. She was the gentlest, ever-caring, overly-concerned and most generous person in my whole life. She was my backbone, my supporter, my life. When my father left us without financial support, my grandmother took in my mother (whom I call Mama), my two brothers and 3-year-old me under her wings.

We were good children, obedient, we never took anything for granted. We were very appreciative of our daily meals and the needs that my grandmother provided for, living from day to day. Now, looking back, I can't imagine how my grandmother survived financially, having only the meagre rental proceeds from three houses that my late grandfather had left her. On top of that, she had responsibilities for her own children, especially my unmarried aunties.

My grandmother was friendly and kind, and she was highly respected in the neighbourhood where we lived. She knew every family that lived along the road, all different races and religions. I remember vividly one incident: there was an elderly single Eurasian lady who lived down the road who was close to my grandmother. When my grandmother received news of her passing away alone in her home, she rushed over, cleaned the deceased and changed her clothes, made sure she looked good, before heading to the local church to ask the priest to take over. I watched this in awe. That was just one of the good deeds she did without any compulsion.

From her, I learned the practice of "Love Thy Neighbours". Living harmoniously irrespective of race, language, culture or religion is the essence of life. This is her legacy which I inherited. I'm gratified to notice that you girls, too, have incorporated this into your lives.

My grandmother emphasised the importance of education. That was her priority for us. Sometimes money was a little tight, but she ensured that we were not deprived of going to school. At times, we went to school without any money for recess, but we didn't bother. Instead, we packed a bun or a plain slice of bread. We lived a simple life of bare necessities, free of pampering and extravagance, yet we were happy.

When I was 10, my youngest brother, then 7, suddenly passed away. That was the first time I learnt what it was to grieve. I was heartbroken to watch Mama crying uncontrollably, hugging my little brother's body during the funeral, and at the same time holding my other brother and me tightly, for fear of losing us next. Asian mothers in those days did not openly express their love to their children. It was the first time I had felt Mama's tight loving hug, and it filled me with emotion. Overnight, I matured. I learnt not to take life and things for granted. I knew it was very difficult for Mama. My brother and I henceforth avoided anything that would hurt or upset Mama.

At a very young age, I envisaged that it would be my responsibility to provide for my grandmother and Mama when I began to work. There was a need to repay my gratitude and appreciation to other family members too, who had supported me during my growing up days.

The words of both my grandmother and Mama still ring in my ears: "Study hard, pass your exams with a certificate, get a good job. That will bring you far, financially." With those words I set my motto and goals: passing exams was important.

I was hardworking in school. I grew up with borrowed books and hand-me-downs from older pupils. I loved reading but couldn't afford to buy story books. I became friendly, or to put it bluntly, mixed with the clever rich kids in my class. These well-to-do kids owned wide selections of story books at home. Being close to them gave me the benefit of borrowing the beautiful array of books their parents could afford for them. In a way I was smart—call it shrewd—in my choice of friends.

However, I made sure I reciprocated their favours, not in material things but in kind, in support and physical aid. It was crucial and important for me to return books borrowed in a timely manner. Henceforth, I learnt that when friends trusted me with their belongings, I had to fulfil that trust. A promise kept was trust fulfilled.

My other source of reading was the newspapers. When I was 8, with dictionary in one hand, my daily routine and reading companion was *The Straits Times*. This was how I gained knowledge and enhanced my choice of vocabulary. Even with this limitation, I enjoyed reading.

So, girls, do you realise that when you were born, your first introduction to toys were books. My love of reading was an influential gift that I imparted to you.

Besides my love of reading, I had this yearning to play the piano. Obviously learning music was beyond my means. Nevertheless, I made the best of it by singing in school concerts, musicals and the choir. My peak experience was being nominated as the school choir conductor, and I was named Best Conductor in an inter-school competition.

Due to my missed opportunity with music, subconsciously, I made music study a must for all of you girls.

I've been a resilient person since I was young; I was independent and strong in facing all hurdles. I didn't need a time-table for my daily routine or studies. I organised my schedule for reading time, homework, studies, and dutifully assisting my grandmother and Mama with household chores. As a Muslim, I readily attended my regular religious classes and daily prayers, obediently.

Why do I share all these with you, girls? I want you to know that I grew up without any wants, nor the extras that other kids enjoyed. Having two good sets of clothes for Eid that lasted till the following year was sheer joy. I took pride in that one pair of shoes my grandmother bought me. I took great care of them so as to make them last as long as they could fit me. Our meals were just rice with either a vegetable dish, or an omelette, or some plain fish. A weekly speciality was a meat dish, with one piece of meat each. It was simple food but it gave us great satisfaction and pleasure. Being "pitiful" never existed for me.

When I was 13, it was the first time I met my father. He was handsome, well-educated with a good job, but he had gone astray. He had returned and reconciled with Mama. Together with Mama we moved to live with him, but with a heavy heart. I missed my grandmother, aunties and uncles who gave us joy in our growing-up days. After this reconciliation, Mama gave birth to a pair of twins (a boy and a girl). Life changed for me tremendously. I had to help with the babies, while toggling with a heavy secondary school workload. Nevertheless, it was my responsibility to continue helping Mama.

Sadly, this complete family life didn't last long. History repeated itself. When I was 17, my father began neglecting us again. In time, Mama went through another divorce. Father died in 1993, in Mecca during pilgrimage. He sought forgiveness from Mama and us before he left, and we forgave him.

I had a dream. I wanted to be successful in life. I wanted to excel in my studies, which I did humbly well till secondary four. Now, with the extra responsibility of caring for the school-going twins, upon completing secondary four, I needed to get a job and support Mama. I yearned to continue for another two years in pre-university (now known as junior college), but we faced financial constraints. To fund my college expenses, I started giving private tuition, every weekend and several evenings after school.

At 17, I was already earning enough to maintain my two-year education. I was a liberated teenager—I could aim for the future I wanted. My twin sister and brother were now beginning to be financially under my care. Mama used to say I was the big sister, the mother and father in the family. I laughed and asked her if that was a compliment or a joke—did I grow old faster than other kids my age?

I knew that immediately upon completing pre-university, I would have to start earning immediately and provide for the family. Therefore, there would be no university for me. At 19, I secured a job in an accounting firm. Fresh from school, inexperienced, I picked up evening courses that related to auditing and accounting. I was enthusiastic. I attended any night classes, including stenography and secretarial skills, that could possibly benefit me, and obtained the certificates. Given this ardour to improve myself, I was never tired of learning.

At 21, my career changed when I joined the banking industry. I embarked on a British correspondence course and obtained a certificate in banking. From this point, I moved up the corporate ladder—from being a clerk in a foreign bank, to an assistant accountant in an investment bank, and finally, at the peak of my career, an associate director (relationship manager) in wealth management for an international bank. I held this position until I retired. Without any university degree, I managed to reach the same position, and I was on par with other university graduates. How did I do it? The answer is sheer hard work, a never-give-up attitude, perseverance in all my different jobs, continuous learning and being positive. I always believed that if others can do it, I too can do it.

A classic example was when I was encouraged to obtain an in-house private banking certificate by my employer. I was 50. I wasn't interested. My thoughts were how could I study at that age? Subsequently, I was assigned to lead a team of 26 staff. One of my duties was to encourage them to sit for this exam. How could I advise my team to do so when I myself didn't do it? Having this responsibility to show a good example, and be a role model to my team, I took the challenge to pass the exam. At 54, after each hard day's work, burning the midnight oil, I embarked on this mission. At that time, I still had responsibilities at home, to look after my unwell Mama, and attend to my late mother-in-law, who was suffering from dementia.

With your Daddy's endless support, I passed the exam. It was definitely an achievement for me. Never underestimate your capabilities. Put your heart into whatever you wish to do genuinely, and you can do it, with God's blessings.

What about marriage? Well, I grew up not knowing any boys, except for my cousins—I studied in a girls' school. With the responsibilities I had inherited, marriage was the last thing on my mind. When I started working, there were several suitors who wished to date me but I avoided them, remembering Mama's broken marriage. Of course there were times I dreamt of having a lovely home of my own, a good, kind man to spend my life with, sitting with my own children at dinnertime, and not worrying for my next day's meals. Yes, I feared most was not having money or losing my job. Paying household bills and providing Mama's welfare was my prime priority. Thus marriage was never on my mind.

It was only when I was 24 that this handsome, soft-spoken, gentleman came into my life and caught my attention—your Daddy. We started to meet up. When he proposed marriage, I asked him candidly, "Are you sure you wish to marry a girl from a broken home?" Knowing my situation, Daddy kindly assured me that he would never stop me from supporting Mama. Thus I got married at 25.

Immediately, after marriage I moved in to stay with my late parents-in-law, to you, Papa and Nanny. For the first time in my life, I tasted what it was like to have a loving father, and a complete, happy family. I was "pre-warned" before marriage by one of Daddy's family members that I would be living with my parents-in-law as they chose to stay with Daddy. I accepted willingly, without any second thoughts. I knew that ultimately, the responsibility would be on Daddy and I to take care of them in their old age. Papa and Nanny were kind and loveable. I looked up to Papa like the father I never had. Several people asked me how was it I could live with my parents-in-laws from day one of my marriage. My answer was: "Your parents-in-law are your elders. Be respectful, polite, accommodating and tolerant. If there was anything that bothered me, I retreated into my room and calmed down. Don't keep any grudges; that is unhealthy and creates hatred. Treat your parents-in-law like you would your own parents. As you live with them, you'll learn how to love them more. Do small things for them like giving them gifts, meals, kind words and caring gestures. They will in turn love you more."

Marriage was good after all. Different from Mama's.

I felt honoured to be the main caregiver to both my parents-in-law and to Mama. I felt it was my duty to take good care of them when they needed me during their twilight years, till they passed away. Taking care of elderly sick persons was not easy. Being a career woman, with three growing children to attend to, the urgencies and requirements of being a caregiver were challenging. One needs much patience. The challenges on my time were unpredictable as the demands from the whole family seemed never-ending. Nevertheless, as Mama had guided me from young to practise "patience is virtue". With that in mind, I became adaptable in my roles: an employee of a top international foreign bank, a caregiver, a mother of three children, and a wife. Something I learnt was never to act irrationally or to be rude when I was upset or when things didn't turn out right. Avoid harsh words that will make you regret later, especially dealing with your loved ones. As a working mother, time management at home was as important, especially in attending to my Mama's and parents-in-law's personal matters and medical appointments. Now I'm retired, I cannot imagine the zest, energy and time I had during those compelling moments in my life.

Bringing you girls up was easy. You were obedient kids who followed the house rules. Yes, your Daddy and I were rather strict. We were frugal and careful with expenses and with your school allowances. We were not extravagant but were generous to those who were in need. You were always there, ever-helpful in taking care of all your grandparents, and several other elders whom I took care of at our place, when they were ill. For that, I salute you girls. You were all very accommodating and responsible. I take pride that you girls have adopted the values that Daddy and I have imparted to you.

Mama was a personification of beauty and patience. She was a replica of my grandmother, kind, generous, ever-smiling, never revealing the hardships she went through, such as parting with the last of her jewellery, just to make ends meet. I admire her strength. She passed away in 2013. After accomplishing my promise to give her the best, happiness and financial comfort, fulfilling my duty as a filial daughter, I decided to retire in 2016.

Retiring at 63? My colleagues and friends were surprised. Of course, like the movie title goes, *Money No Enough*. Nothing in this world is enough. However, there are some things you can't buy: family time and health. Yes, I wanted to spend more time with the family, especially with your Daddy, more so since we are both now at the prime of our age. I too wish to spend as much time as possible with your kids, my little darling grandchildren, and to be there when

Granny's help is needed. With retirement I also managed to allocate more time to spirituality, as well as to community and volunteer work. It is now my time.

In conclusion, my girls, most important is to have a good character, to be polite, respectful, compassionate and non-judgemental. Lead an honest, truthful life. Never lie nor cheat, it will bring disaster. Set this as the foundation of your life. Do seek forgiveness when you are wrong and to forgive the one who is wrong is divine. This will bring you inner peace and happiness. Remember, our actions speak louder than words.

I say this to any kid who comes from a broken home: there is no excuse to be a failure in your life. Life is a journey. Make the best of any limitation or obstacle thrown at you. Through this letter, I'm imparting my lifetime experience that has moulded me into what I am today. My life is almost complete but my chapter is not closed yet.

Yes, this is the girl from a broken family. Do I look broken?

Love always,
Mummy

KALTHUM AHMAD started her career in an accounting/auditing/share registration firm in February 1973. In 1974, she switched careers to banking, an industry she remained in until her retirement in 2016. Throughout her 43 years in banking she has had experiences in foreign banks as well as a merchant/investment bank. Her last position, which she held for 21 years, was in wealth management with a renowned foreign private bank. Throughout her life, Kalthum has been actively engaged in voluntary work. Now in her retirement, she is helping with senior-related programmes and assisting in an educational programme for underprivileged children in primary schools. Kalthum loves reading, singing, dramas and poetries. She is wife to a loving husband, mother of three beautiful daughters aged 41, 38 and 36, and a doting grandmother of seven lovely grandchildren, aged between 1 and 14.

Kalthum Ahmad and her three daughters when they were young.

How You Became My Daughter

Lin Xiuzhen

Hi Zara,

This is being written when you are 4 years old. I am not sure when you will read this letter, but I believe by the time you do, you will be able to understand what "adopted" means.

When you were very young, almost since birth, you have been told this and have heard us saying this. I have always told you that you did not come from Mummy's tummy but from an angel, but I am not sure if you understand what it means even now.

You are very, very special to us. Our journey with you begun way before you came into our arms, way before the pregnancy began. I would like to tell you your story.

In March 2014, Papa and I went on a mission trip together to Iloilo, a province in the Philippines. It was the first time we signed up for and served on a mission together. It was also the first medical mission for both of us.

It was very different from our usual mission trips; we had to work in a medical post in various slum areas, setting up blood pressure stations, conducting consultations and issuing medication to those who were sick or injured.

In one slum area, we saw a cute little girl—we both fell in love with her. I visited her at her home, which was a tiny wooden hut. There was just enough space for a queen size bed—there was no walking space and the family all had to squeeze together to sleep.

On that mission trip, we gave out toys and stationery to those kids in the slum areas, and so we gave this little girl a teddy bear. That was the first time the seed was sown in our hearts to adopt, to love and to raise up a child.

But at the time, there were many things happening at home. Your Grandmother and Grandfather—whom you have never met—were struggling with cancer, and Papa and I were visiting them in hospital almost weekly. So we were not sure if we could commit to and be emotionally capable of giving our fullest love and support to a child.

At the end of 2015, both your grandparents ended their fight with cancer and finally went to be with Jesus. It was not an easy time for Papa and me, and we took time to find rest in God.

One day in May 2016, I asked Papa if he felt he wanted to and was ready to adopt a child. I told Papa to take time to pray about this decision. In June 2016, I went to Iloilo again on another medical mission. This time, Papa was not there with me. When I visited the same slum and saw this girl, she had grown up to be a beautiful little girl in the two years we had not seen each other. She remembered me and came to look for me.

I took a photo with the girl and sent it to Papa. He asked if the girl would like to come to Singapore. I would have loved to adopt her, but the decision had to be made by the man of the house, so I told Papa to think and pray about it before we decided.

During that second trip, I visited more houses in the slum. The children all lived in cramped spaces, and they lacked education because their parents had no financial ability to send them to school. Some of the children were abandoned, left to fend for themselves. The human trafficking rate was high in that place. From that experience, God placed in us the desire to provide a family and a home for a child.

We started exploring how we could adopt a child. After much research and speaking to different authorities, we discovered that Singaporeans are not allowed to adopted from the Philippines. Singaporeans are only allowed to adopt from a few countries and Malaysia is one of them.

After praying and talking things through, I spoke to my spiritual mentor who encouraged me to go for it. She also linked me up with a couple who adopted. This couple shared with us the adoption process, and recommended that we attend an adoption workshop to find out more, and to see if we were really prepared to become adoptive parents.

The more we researched, the greater our desire to adopt grew. Not because we felt our family was incomplete without a child. Papa and I were quite happy to dote on the children of our good friends. As a family without children, we were also happy the way we were. But throughout all this time, I felt that God was divinely directing us to something He had prepared for us and for you.

Baby Zara, our beautiful daughter, you are adopted and you are now our daughter forever. As much as you bring us joy, we pray that we will be godly parents to you and provide for you, bringing you up in the way and the fear of the Lord.

Though you did not come to us the usual way—from my tummy after a nine-month journey—I believe you are God's perfect answer to the prayer that Papa and I prayed. I believe

Xiuzhen and her daughter Zara.

you have always been in the plan of God for us, right from the very beginning, even before you were formed and brought to us through an angel.

The waiting process was not easy—we endured the constant changes and uncertainty about your outcome. But somehow, we just knew deep in our hearts that God had reserved you for us, and it had always been you, right from the beginning.

In the Bible, it says in Romans 8:28, "All things works together for the good for those we love Him and are called according to His purpose."

As you grow up, you will know that you have been written about on my blog, featured in media stories about adoption. I want you to know that I chose not to hide the fact that you are adopted, because I want you to know that I will never, not for one moment, be ashamed or embarrassed of you! And not for a moment would I ever want you to feel that we are not proud of you!

You are not an accident. You are beautifully and wonderfully made in the image of God. You are chosen, an elect, destined to be placed into this family and into God's house.

You are mine and I am yours. You will have everything I planned and reserved for my child. Nothing less. We have been falling in love with you since we first saw you, and every single day after.

Yes, as you grow up, you may feel that Mama is always strict with you, but I just want you to know that I love you. I love you just as I have from the beginning. I promised to go into your room every night to kiss you good night and I will still do it even when you are asleep. You are loved, by us and all our family and friends—everyone has loved you as our own.

I pray that your journey with us will not be something you will ever be ashamed of or feel that you need to hide from the world, but that it will be your very own testimony to tell the world how God has chosen you from the beginning and placed His destiny in your life, to shine for Him and to glorify Him.

Love,
Mama

LIN XIUZHEN is a resin artist, graphic designer, painter and entrepreneur. She has been a freelance graphic designer since 2007. Xiuzhen founded The Last Piece Sg at Haji Lane in 2015 and took over fashion blogshop MissyStella & Co in 2016. She was commissioned to create resin art pieces for ST Signature Chinatown Hotel at Tras Street. Her art pieces also retail at Kensington Square. Xiuzhen co-founded The Common Good in 2020, an event space for corporate events which also serves as workshop space for art, art jamming and dance events. She also co-founded The Space Artistry Pte Ltd, an interior design company that offers design and space planning services.

Mommy's Running Chronicles

Loretta Urquhart

I still remember the day I started running. I woke up on Christmas morning in 2008, a single mom, and decided that I needed to do something in my life for me. I pondered over all the numerous activities that I could do; art classes, dance lessons, the gym, the list went on.

Ultimately, I figured that all subscriptions would be a waste of money, since we live right across the beach. That day, for the first time in my life, I decided that I would run.

You have to understand that it was not an easy decision, having struggled with the stigma of being an overweight teenager. The first few times I tried, I could barely run for 50 metres without panting, but it felt extremely liberating too. It felt like the first steps to embracing real change in my life. Running is tough—you need stamina, energy, endurance and mental perseverance to push yourself to complete the round, as well as do it daily. In all honesty, I often had to use many wildly imaginative scenarios in my head to motivate myself to keep pushing forward. I imagined

I was keeping up with hunky tattooed guys (which I never did). I imagined was doing a slo-mo run like in *Chariots Of Fire*. I even imagined I was Rocky, running as *Eye Of The Tiger* played in the background. For someone who had not done a single bit of exercise in all of 42 years of living, I managed to clock seven kilometres within a span of five months. (I decided to stop at seven since seven rhymes with heaven and that felt right to me.)

Since that day, running has become a daily religion to me and I have not stopped, even throughout my treatments as I was battling cancer. I thought angels had given me wings to fly. Every time I ran, I could compartmentalise and reflect on my happiness, sadness, disappointments and everything else I have experienced in my life. It allowed my creative brainwaves to flow freely and manifest ideas in my head. It is because of my commitment to running that I truly believe that no problem is too big to handle. While you run, you learn to pace your steps, use breathing techniques and move effectively—all of which can be lessons applied to the rest of your life and how you learn to handle it. You have to learn to run at your own pace, in the same way you approach your own journey in life. Things only can happen in time but you need to have the dedication and set goals to achieve it. It is only apt then, that as I express my thoughts and affection in a letter for my two lovely girls, that I would use my journey through running as a way to chronicle my life journey.

To my girls: I hope these five lessons can bring some enlightenment and encouragement to both of you as you commence on your journey into adulthood, with or without Mommy.

The First and Second Kilometres: Cherish the moments

It's always exhilarating to take that first step after planning the running route. I think about the folks I will meet, as well as the smiles and waves I might give and receive along the journey.

As an expectant mom, I had numerous dreams and aspirations about how I would raise my kids. I always knew there would be two children as I felt it would be nice to have a fellow sibling to rely on throughout the years. I am fortunate to be blessed with you two wonderful girls, both sharing so many similarities while yet simultaneously being individuals in your own capacities.

Both of you arrived prematurely, delivered naturally just before noon and weighing two kilograms, with a three year divide between you two. But the similarities end there. Ainsley was born with a pinkish complexion and curly ginger-red hair while Keisia was born tan with a full head of ebony hair. Your personalities were different too; Ainsley always sported a daredevil grin that complimented her gregarious personality, while Keisia was quiet and preferred to just stick around Mommy, holding on like a little koala.

But even as toddlers, both girls had hearts of gold: you learnt the art of generosity that it is better to give than to receive. It may have been something as simple as offering candy or chocolates to your friends, even though there were definitely times I remember when you would be sad as there was none left for you. It was then I reminded you to remember the smiles your friends left, explaining that there was no need to be selfish as Mommy could get some more.

Parenthood was not an easy task for a working mom. Mornings were absolute madness—I woke up early, rushed to strap Ainsley in a baby carrier and bolted down the sidewalk in killer heels to catch two different buses so I could drop her off at Grand-Aunty's home. The bus was crowded but Ainsley enjoyed every single journey, constantly smiling and waving at anyone who would give us kindness, be it another smile or a seat offered to us. Those bus rides back then were priceless bonding moments that I remember fondly, because I spent so much time singing and talking to you.

Looking back, I regret that I did not get the same daily bus ride experience with Keisia. When I later traded my life insurance endowment plan for a car instead, life became a blur of constant rushing as we always had somewhere to get to. Though car rides made the morning routine significantly easier, it just was not the same as the bus rides. Perhaps this is also the reason why Keisia became Mommy's girl, so much so that her favourite phrase when she was unhappy would be "I tell my Mommy!"

So my advice to both of you for when you have children next time is this: take time to cherish the moments together, especially the toddler years. It is far too easy to forget to appreciate your time together and before you know it, they have suddenly all grown up. Babies grow too quickly.

The Third Kilometre: Purge the despair
I am still running on a high at the third kilometre, moving at a constant rhythm, feeling so awesome after breaking the first couple of milestones.

As your Mom, I wanted to show you the world as I experienced it: life is not always a gentle bed of roses. I grew up having to fight for everything I believed in, whether it was with friends or relatives. I hope to impart the same fighting spirit in both of you.

Your Grandpa was adopted as a baby, and I came to understand the harsher realities of the world as a young child, often through the many injustices that fell upon him. His marriage to your Grandma was not appreciated or approved by either side of the family because he is Peranakan while she is Hainanese. Even worse was the religion your Grandpa chose to embrace, Catholicism, which your Grandma also adopted. It was considered inappropriate and offensive.

Growing up, I encountered mixed and conflicting cultures, even down to the most basic of eating with fingers or fork and spoon in one household, versus chopsticks in the other. While it was fun to visit my Popo's home, the visit sometimes ended with me in tears as my uncle would question me repeatedly about my beliefs. I was only 5 years old, but he would relentlessly ask me questions like "Who made you?", and when I reply "God did!" he would debunk it by saying that it was my parents.

But, in a way, I am glad to have those experiences since I believe this was what shaped me as a person. At such a young age, I was already able to hold onto my thoughts clearly, learn to ignore unkind words, injustice and things that were way beyond my control. You should never be afraid to stand up for what you believe in, but you must also know that some things and people will always be stubborn. Never let that stop you.

Life is sometimes weird and unpredictable and you don't necessarily always reap what you sow. The key phrase here is "Life's not fair", which is something I had to learn as a child. When I had just turned 13, Grandpa passed away, and suddenly everything changed. It felt like we became poor overnight. Beyond going to school, my sister and I had to fend for ourselves at home while your grandma went to work at the factory. Each month we queued at St Vincent de Paul for our monthly food rations, which gave me such strange feelings of helplessness and embarrassment whenever I bumped into my friends at church during 'Collection Sunday'. The uncomfortable stigma of being poor is something that I will always keep with me, and something I swore in my heart that I would never bestow on my kids.

When I started to work after graduation, I had to endure constant berating and rhetorical nonsense from my insecure supervisors. These things often happen when you are an entry level employee, but I felt it was often more so for someone like me since I always seemed to stand out from the clutter. In everything I do, I refuse to toe the line and am never afraid to speak up my mind. The way I see it is that, when you have hit rock bottom, nothing else can beat you down except yourself, so why not just stand up and fight? When I was faced with injustice at work, which ultimately led to my resignation, I am glad that I never allowed the experience to eat into my own work ethics.

I believe that, in order to appreciate the goodness in life, you need to experience ugliness. There is always a time and a place for everything. God is great, and He has been good to me. I was a late bloomer in my career but when it started to soar, it moved in leaps and bounds, especially after the divorce. I guess I needed to purge the unpleasantness to redirect my focus.

The Fourth and Fifth Kilometres: I admire your resilience amidst my struggles

At about the fourth kilometre my run is becoming a struggle now; the midway point is generally where you start to experience fatigue. As I adjust my breathing and work to maintain the speed there are many times I mentally wish the rain would fall so I have to cut my run short. Life is like that too—things happen and when it gets difficult sometimes you just want to hit eject. Giving up is never the worthwhile option, which is why at this point I keep running, and I run harder.

I am glad that I was never the typical mom who coddled both of you with endless attention. As toddlers you quickly learnt that crying was not tolerated by me, even when you fell down. The only exception to that rule would be when there was blood, or if someone passed away. (Even today, I still do not tolerate tears very well.) But more importantly, I am happy that I raised and prepared both of you to become independent young women.

With me being a busy single mom, both of you frequently had to summarise all your school forms and report them to me at the dinner table while I worked. Sometimes I remember you girls were even able to make important school decisions on your own in advance, only needing my signed consent on the form. Looking back, I am thankful that both of you learnt courage, confidence and maturity at such a young age.

The separation from your dad and divorce dragged on for many years, and it took a serious toll on all of us. I, in particular, was lost in depression for slightly over a year, with zero or little recollection of how you girls coped. What I do remember, thankfully, are your smiles, as both of you always tried to cheer me up in your own little ways.

Ainsley, you probably suffered the most during the divorce as you had to become the adult in the house and take care of Keisia. You often reminded me of which day I had to be at her kindergarten for concerts or parent-teacher meetings. You learnt to be discreet and subtle in the words you chose, careful to not say things that would upset me. No words can really describe how truly sorry I am.

Often I feel like a failure—how can I succeed in so many things in life but fail so miserably at marriage? But also, it takes two to tango and if there was ever something I could change, I would have removed your Dad from my life sooner and taken all those horrible memories away. I think what I admire most is how you girls learnt to stick together as sisters. I would like to believe that perhaps my strict mentoring was a large contributor to your resilience today.

The Sixth Kilometre: I'm impressed that you have a vision

Hitting the sixth kilometre while running highlights the feel of the headwind and relief. With the end in sight, it becomes much easier to slowly accelerate your pace and move in purpose, just like in life.

I am so proud of you, Ainsley and Keisia. Despite the strife and setbacks during your growing years, both of you have grown to be level-headed girls with a strong vision and focus on what you want to achieve in life.

Despite the constant debates I had with Keisia about her passion for baking, and my doubts about the viability of her goals, she never once wavered in the pursuit of her dreams. This determination remains even till today, as she is interning in a Michelin-star restaurant, and I am incredibly proud that she remained steadfast in her wish regardless of the pushback she has received.

As for Ainsley, this smart cookie has always been capable of doing anything she wanted in life but had to navigate a difficult emotional battle during her teenage years. Nevertheless, today I sit here intoxicated with pride—Ainsley, you managed to overcome it and emerge stronger! With each day you are already one step closer to realising your dreams and I am delighted to be part of that.

Most importantly, my victory over cancer would not have been possible if I did not have both girls by my side cheering me on. So I just want to say: stay focused and never lose sight of your goals as I do with my running, but also with every challenge I encounter in my life. The journey ahead will be long, full of challenges but each milestone will be worth it, I promise you. When it comes to a point where you can look back and measure your progress, you will feel that same exhilaration as I have felt: the feeling that you have beaten the odds despite it all.

The Seventh Kilometre: Humour in life

As I approach the finishing line, the sense of achievement overwhelms me – I feel alive! I thank God always for my Speedy Gonzales spirit to run.

When I look back at the years we've spent together so far, I recognise that it has been fraught with difficulty and filled with heart-breaking moments. As a mother—your mother—I curse at what life has brought you. Though I feel that both of you have experienced the harsh realities of life too soon, in many ways I am still grateful that at the end of the day, we got through these moments together. These experiences have brought us extremely close together creating a mother-daughter-sister bond so strong that no distance will be able to truly divide us. Even today we still constantly have our endless chatter and crazy laughing moments that I will always cherish.

Humour in life is important. It helps us to overcome challenges. Falling is not so hard when you can simply laugh and get up again. I ask that you remember how I would tease you both, saying that I picked you up from the trash bin, even walking to the supposedly place I had "found" you. Remember the moments when I got so upset that I threatened to flush Keisia down the toilet. To my horror this feisty soul would later threaten the same thing to a kindergarten friend, which prompted an invitation to the principal's office to discuss Keisia's "mental state".

I am so glad that both of you can laugh at yourselves and are comfortable poking fun at each other. Life is hard enough as it is, there is no need to take everything so seriously; it makes me happy that we are able to find joy regardless of what happens. There is so much to cherish in our lives together and I look forward to continued adventures with both of you.

These runs follow a similar journey to life: you discover your goals, you struggle, you fall, you learn to improve.

Measuring the progress is crucial to keep yourself on your toes, you learn to focus and strive for more. You think: "I want to go out and run with a bang! I want to reach a new personal best!" My competitive nature in running is one and the same as my vision in life. It brings me great joy and satisfaction, which I wish on the both of you as well. One day, many moons from now, whenever you see someone running, I hope you will remember my running chronicles dedicated to both of you.

I love you loads always,
Mommy

Loretta (centre) with Ainsley and Keisia.

A relentless alchemist of integrated marketing and communications solutions, **LORETTA URQUHART'**s unwavering dedication to continually think out of the box and create outstanding results in her field of work has seen her achieving goals and targets for the companies throughout her career. From developing media strategies, being a spokesperson, to organising high profile events and product launches, Loretta is firm in her approach to that diligence and embodies the ability to unlearn, relearn and learn. Outside of work, the mother of two unwinds by cooking, running and shopping.

To Be A Mother Is The Best Decision I Ever Made

Dawn Lee

Dear Denise and Debbie,

When I considered writing this letter, I had a lot of things on my mind. I had many ideas about how I should present this, but I ended up not knowing what to say—is this a brain jam? Maybe it's the perfectionist in me that wanted to leave both of you a perfect letter from your Mom. But after resting my mind for a few days, I realized that there is only one thing I want both of you to know, and it is that I love you very much.

Being your mother is one of the best decisions that I have made in my life. My mother, your Grandma, left me when I was 11 years old. I grew up in a family where my Dad, your Grandpa, was on overseas assignments most of the time.

As far as I could remember, when my Dad came home from overseas, he would bring us presents. Unfortunately, I also remember when he was home, many quarrels would take place at home between him and my mother. There were times where Grandma would leave home for days and she would only come back when Grandpa asked her to.

This cycle went on for years, until finally, one day, Grandpa gave up on the marriage and decided not to ask Grandma to come home. Overnight, my paternal grandmother, your Great-grandmother, shifted in with us and took over the responsibilities of looking after Auntie Mel and me.

So you can say that I grew up without a mother figure. At the age of 11, I had to learn to be independent. Grandpa continued to travel for work. Unlike today, where kids are more tech-savvy and avenues of communication are readily available, Auntie Mel and me were never in touch with our mother after she left.

Even though Great-grandmother was supposed to take care of us, in many ways, we had to grow up and take care of her and the household. Life went on for another four years like this, until Auntie Mel decided to move out at the age of 16. This was the second time I lost a female figure in my life. Grandpa was heartbroken but there was nothing he could do to keep Auntie Mel.

These two incidents made a huge impact in my life, even though I was not aware of it at the time. I began to think that woman are not dependable, that they cannot be trusted. That they will leave and abandon you. I had to learn to fend for myself. Now that I looked back, I realised that I struggled very much with low self-esteem. Even though I was doing well academically in school and I had many friends, I often felt that I was not good enough, pretty enough, or smart enough. Thoughts that maybe people were just being nice to me, or that I didn't belong to any group would often creep into my mind.

I started to do sports and I strived to excel at them. I played basketball and was selected for the combined schools team and the national team. I joined the track and field team and came in fourth at the national level. I played netball and volleyball. I even joined the English Language Drama Society and tried to act.

But all these did not fill the void in my heart. I didn't have relationships because my self-esteem was so low that I did not think that any boy would be interested in me. Even if boys expressed interest in me, I was probably not confident enough to pick up the signal. So now you know why your Dad was my first boyfriend when I was 22.

My life took a turn for the better when I came to church at 16. I found myself in an environment where people accepted me and loved me for who I was. I learnt to love God, to love myself and to love others. Of course, the hardest thing for me was to learn to love my mother and sister who left me. I thank God that many people came around me to help me in this journey of inner healing. I went through many prayer and counseling sessions. It was like peeling onions, removing layers and layers of past hurts and disappointments. Over the years, I had allowed the past to plant that fear of abandonment in me and I did not know how to deal with it—until I met God.

By the grace of God, my mother and I finally reconciled after many years. What both of you see today is the result of the healing that God has done for me in my life. He showed me that He forgave a sinner like me and I can, in turn, forgive a mother who had left me because she did not know better. God had a way of orchestrating our lives—just as He gave my mother two daughters, He also gave me two beautiful daughters!

Two years after your Dad and I got married, we felt that it was time to bring our marriage to the next level, which was to start a family. Perhaps I was young, at 28, I conceived quickly. It was very exciting to be a first-time mum. We were initially happy to stop at one child. However, three years later, we felt that life isn't complete without siblings. That's when Debbie, you came along.

Life can never prepare a woman to be a mother. The role and responsibilities drop on you the moment the little one decides to pop into this world. There is no one-size-fits-all solution to raising your children. Every child is unique and not even having a PhD can help you to raise one. But one thing's for sure: a mother's love is instinctive and powerful.

When both of you were infants, my life totally revolved around you. Your first turn, first tooth, first solids, first words, first steps… I wanted to be there to witness all these. At some point, even though we hired a domestic helper, I was a very hands-on mother. My hair was constantly out of shape because I had no time for regular haircuts. I traded office wear for comfy oversized clothes because I was totally out of shape after delivery. Exercise was the last thing on my mind because as a mother, I did not make time for myself. My world was you.

I stopped wearing make-up because I carried each of you in a sling against my chest and I wanted to avoid smudging you with make-up. My days started early with your food preparation and packing your baby bags. I gave up wearing heels because it was just impossible to walk in them when I had my work bag on one shoulder, a baby bag on the other and a baby hanging in front of me. Both times, each of you became the only accessory that I needed in my life. And I was most proud to "hang" you all over me.

Both your Dad and I came from a family of four: parents and two kids. There are so many reasons why we think siblings are important. But the great one is that siblings are the gift only your parents—and no-one else in this world—can give to you. Someone once said, "Sisters are the best friend you never had". My hope is that both of you will grow in your love for each other. Blood is thicker than water. Learn to get along. Both of you may be so different, but you are also very similar in many ways.

Aunty Mel and I resumed our relationship many years later. She was promoted to the status of "Auntie" when both of you were born. I saw her through her first marriage and divorce, and now she is happily married to Uncle Chiheb. I walked with her when she was battling leukemia—I was so disappointed that my bone marrow did not match hers. Fortunately, she did not need one.

One of my best overseas holidays was touring Italy with Auntie Mel. It was my first time in Europe—and I'll be honest to say that the best thing was that she paid for the entire trip! She trusts me with all her finances. She would consult me before making major decisions in life. Now that she has relocated to Tunisia, both of you know that we still communicate with each other very often and hold each other dearly in our hearts.

Love yourself. You are the best gift that your parents could ever give to your sister.

Love your sister. She is the only gift that your parents and no one else can ever give to you.

I have enjoyed watching both of you grow into your teenage years, and I will eventually enjoy watching you enter adulthood. Sometimes I wish that I can keep you small so that you will always stay by our side, but I also know that there are so many adventures we can share together when you are adults. Even now, there are things I already miss.

I miss the times you would call me every day during recess time. I used to think that it was a waste of money and you should have saved the 10 cents.

I miss the times both of you would sleep with us on our bed. I used to say it's to save electricity so that we only switch on one air conditioner at night. But secretly, I enjoyed having both of you snuggling between us.

Every growing phase is a passing phase and I have learnt to enjoy every moment before it is gone. Life is about creating memories. So we travel together, we eat together, laugh together, watch silly YouTube videos together. I want to be part of your world for as long as I can.

When I tell you, you cannot go overseas with your friends, what I really mean is, "If you want to see the world, let me go with you."

When I say, do not find a boyfriend too soon, what I really mean is, "I want you to be my little girl as long as you can and I do not want another person to take my place in your heart."

When I ask, will you stay with me after you are married? What I want to know is how far away you will be after marriage.

It is going to be difficult, but I know I will need to let you go someday.

So what do I want to leave with you? Life is about making choices and it is okay to make wrong choices or mistakes in life—just don't make the same mistake twice. What is worse than making a wrong choice is not having a choice.

I hope that you do not come to a place where you have to make a choice because you have no choice. Pursue God, gain knowledge, live an honest life. The better you do in life, the more choices you will have in life. Education and money may not be the most important pursuits in life, but a higher education will lead you to more career choices. Choose a career that will eventually become your passion. Then you are not paid for working, but you will be paid for doing something you enjoy. Do not be afraid of hardship and huge tasks. As the saying goes: How do you eat an elephant? One bite at a time. You will make choices about the house you live in, the car you drive, the job you choose and the guy you marry. Life is about choices.

So my advice to you is, choose wisely.

There are three most important decisions you need to make in life: one, your salvation; two, the Church you choose to grow in; three, the guy you marry.

Someone once said just because you are born in McDonalds, that does not make you a hamburger. Just because both of you are born into a Christian family, it does not make you a believer. I pray that both of you walk closely with God. There have been prophecies that were spoken into your lives and I know that the Lord is watching over both of you. I pray that Dad and I can leave a spiritual legacy for you and your descendants to come.

Lastly, marriage can either be a heaven on earth, or hell on earth. Make many friends. Draw boundaries. Take your time to choose wisely. Do not look for the right one; make the one that you choose right. Remember that marriage is hard work. If you are not willing to put in effort to make it work, then do not get married. Every person in a marriage must first love God, love himself or herself, and lastly, love their spouse.

It is important that you choose someone who shares the same values as you. If he loves God, he will love you. Love yourself; you will be disappointed if you are waiting for someone to love you. True beauty comes from being confident in who you are. You are not what you weigh so do not be overly pressured into conforming to what this world thinks a pretty woman should look like.

Are you willing to forgo the entire forest for a single tree? Take your time to look for that "tree". For richer or poorer, in sickness and in health; take your time to choose that person whom you are willing to go through life with. I hope our marriage has been an example to you. I hope we have shown you that in the midst of any differences, you can still make your marriage work if you are willing to commit to your wedding vows.

When that day comes for you to get married, I will cry buckets. I will try to remind myself that you need to "leave and cleave". It will be difficult, but I will try because that is what the Bible says. Sigh. But I will remind myself that as a mother, my children never really leave me because I forever hold them dearly in my heart.

In closing, I want to reiterate that I love both of you very much. When I tell you that you can have my cup of bubble tea in the fridge or the last piece of sweet and sour pork

Dawn with her daughters Denise and Debbie.

at dinner, I am not just giving you permission to drink or eat—giving you my bubble tea and letting you have the last piece of pork is my way of telling you that I love you more than my desires.

When you ask if you can buy something and most of the time, I say no, what I mean is, I love you, let me buy for you later. You know that I hate to say no to both of you.

As a mother, I have learnt that I am capable of loving others more than myself and I am willing to sacrifice for others, especially my children.

As a mother, I discovered that I am really a superhero in disguise because I possess super memory power and can handle many tasks all at one time.

Thank you for coming into my life. I cannot imagine life without the both of you! When they say babies are bundle of joy, I did not expect that it would mean so much joy! The

Bible says children are gifts from heaven. I thank God that He gave both of you to me.

I look forward to the day both of you become mothers and have children of your own.

Love,
Mom

DAWN LEE is married to Daniel and is mother to two teenage daughters, Denise and Debbie—they are the D Family! Dawn is a full-time working mother—she is neither an ambitious career woman nor a stay-home mom, but she enjoys the challenge of juggling both work and wife-mum responsibilities. Dawn is also an athlete, her favorite race being a triathlon which lets her swim, cycle and run. To her, life is an adventure, and her motto is to "live a day at a time".

Part 3

THE BABY GIRL GROWS UP

"No daughter and mother ever live apart, no matter
what the distance between them."
—Christie Watson

Humility, Grit And The Family Business

Janet Goh

My dearest Rachel,

What a wonderful 21 years I've had with you.

I love the day you came into my life: the sleepless nights because you cried and I didn't know why; the smelly diapers I changed and those fevers that finally broke after three days. I remember the resolve on your face, at the tender age of 16 months, when you decided that you did not need diapers anymore, and our tearful farewell on your first day in Nursery. I recall your enthusiasm at school campfires; the injuries you bore from your hockey games and the three exciting times when we collected your national examination results.

Then, there was the first of our many fights, the moments we agree to disagree. Your fascination with nails, hair, make-up and fashion. Our holidays without the boys. Your relationships highs and lows.

Such precious moments are these.

I know that it has not been an easy ride for you, especially during your teenage years, but through sheer grit, you have risen above the challenges, the curveballs that Life has thrown at you. I love you immeasurably and I'm so proud of you, baby girl!

As you start your academic year, embrace the new normal of e-learning and social distancing during this period of COVID-19. Of course, these are not the ideal circumstances for your final year but we must learn to adapt and to evolve. Open book and online exams that give you extended time to complete, if taken with the right attitude, test not just head knowledge but also your integrity and discipline, which is critical in "adulting".

Circumstances like these draw you out of your comfort zone and it is often in times of crises that you will see exponential growth in character and strength. This is also a time of reflection: focus on what you have and how you can make the most of your limited resources. Stay informed and keep an eye and ear out for changes in your industry of choice. Continue to put your best efforts into the modules you will take regardless whether the grades count toward your degree or not. Focus on the process of learning, so that you will graduate not simply with a good certificate, but with a growth mindset that is poised to explore, to learn from successes and failures and to strive for excellence in all your endeavours.

Seeing how you have developed, from the time you had to decide which course to take, to your choice of destination for your overseas exchange programme; and most recently, the company you chose to spend six months doing an internship with, assures me that your motivation is not only money. For that I am relieved.

Instead of taking the easy way out, you had researched and explored the various options that would enable you to marry your interests and passion with your education. You have also availed yourself to job opportunities in related fields during your semestral holidays, keeping yourself relevant and productive. I am further impressed that when you want to pick up a skill, you practise till you perfect it. This is seen in how you can now do your own beautiful nail art, and how you started your own home bakery business last year, catering to themed parties. I am confident that your hard work and tenacity will be rewarded in good time.

Perhaps you have already mentally laid out your career path and progression. But the effects of the pandemic on the economy have derailed your plans. Do not be discouraged. You are not alone in this situation and the world is ever changing. Bad times will improve and new opportunities will present themselves. In the meantime, the best thing we can do is upgrade ourselves, tighten our belts and press on.

When you start your career, be mindful that a humble attitude is key. Listen attentively and observe more. Think before you speak and be intentional in your learning. No need for regrets—accept that mistakes will be made at some point in time, but you must take quick responsibility for your actions, reflect and most importantly, learn from it. Then move forward. Never try to cover up or hope that a mistake will die a natural death. It never does, and it is more likely to come back and haunt you when you least expect it! When you achieve success and wealth, continue to spend within your means and do not underestimate its effect on your character. You have to constantly remind yourself to stay grounded and not get sucked in by arrogance and materialism. Be beautiful inside out.

As you know, the family business has sustained us all these years. Although I do not push you to join us, it does not mean that I do not want you in the business or that your contribution is not valued. Gong Gong started the business because he figured that as he did not have a lot money to leave as inheritance for your aunt, uncle and I, starting a business would give the three of us the opportunity to be our own bosses, and thereby create our own wealth.

I joined the company upon graduation because the business was just starting out then and we needed all hands on board. At that time, it was not a matter of choice but a decision borne of necessity. There are many benefits to running your own show: we have the flexibility of time and there is no need to worry about clocking in the hours. However, as an owner, you have a vested interest in the performance of the company, you are always thinking, eating and sleeping the business. It may sound like a lot of work but the job satisfaction rating is right up there!

Naturally, your Gong Gong would be ecstatic should you want to join us as your two cousins living in America have chosen TO. Your aunt and I felt that while it was important for us to encourage all of you to pursue your dreams, we need also to "sell" our company to you and present all the facts and benefits for your consideration. Know that when you are a business owner, you are directly rewarded for your efforts; it is not diluted through various levels of management. Your decision-making process is also simpler and straightforward without having to be passed through layers of approval. We believe that your resourceful and tech savvy generation would be able to take full advantage of the infrastructure that we have established and use it to bring the company to new heights.

However, I believe that business dealings are not everyone's cup of tea. Forcing a square peg into a round hole would be detrimental to our business and may adversely affect our relationship. Therefore, I want you to make the decision for yourself based on what is best for you, and not because you feel obligated to be that third generation owner, or because joining the family business is the path of least resistance.

While your Gong Gong is a strong and determined businessman, your late Ah Ma, on the other hand, was a gentle, kind and compassionate woman. I have learnt so much from them, and so can you.

Gong Gong had nine younger sisters. He did not complete his secondary education as he had to leave school and work to help support the family. During that time, he did not give up on learning and simply worked hard to improve his English vocabulary by reading a dictionary. Once he had a reasonably good reservoir of words, he continued reading any book he could lay his hands on. Eventually, through reading self-help books, he obtained his skills in business and people management. In same way, he became fluent in Mandarin and learnt Bahasa Indonesia from scratch. Gong Gong worked as a salesman and when we were growing up, he was a sales manager in a multi-national company, which was a pretty big deal back then for an Asian man without a formal education.

As for your late Ah Ma, it is sad that you did not have the chance to spend much time with her as we moved to Hong Kong when you were little, and she passed away while we were still living there. Your Ah Ma was a kind, gentle and compassionate woman. She was generous with her time and resources, and was ever ready to sprint into action to help anyone out. Her take on life was that we must never pander to the rich or influential, but rather, our time should be spent extending help to those who are in need and less fortunate than we are. Apart from her hair which had to be perfectly coiffed at all times, she was simple and content.

Today, technology has made learning resources easily accessible. We need to take advantage of it to constantly improve ourselves. As you can learn from Gong Gong, reading the right books will give you the knowledge needed to achieve your goals. It will increase and deepen your understanding on any topic of interest and it can train your mind to effectively analyse situations. All in all, reading can set you up for success.

While you push forward to achieve your goals and dreams, remain kind and compassionate, not just with your words but also by your actions. Prioritise people, not things; because no matter how busy we are, there will always be time for what you prioritise. Be fair in your dealings and do not take advantage of anyone. Be grateful, not entitled. Keep in mind the kindness that others have shown you, so that you will also look out for opportunities to extend the same to others.

Everyone has a life story to tell. Our characters and personalities are often shaped by our reactions to circumstances in our lives. So be like your Ah Ma: choose to give everyone the benefit of doubt and simply act in kindness regardless of how you are treated by them. (But be sensible—I'm not suggesting that you be gullible and fall prey to cheats.) Giving from the heart brings inexplicable joy and peace.

There will be moments in life you will be disappointed by a situation, relationship or lost opportunity. You will feel hurt and you may feel like you don't want to get out of bed. In those instances, don't. Stay in bed. Give yourself a limited time to grief, wallow, fume—whatever. But when all that is done, get up, wash up and know that you are precious to your family who loves you, especially me. Know that your worth is not defined by that hurt or disappointment.

Rachel dear, I appreciate all the fights that we have had. We are both extremely emotional and our voices increase in volume with every statement when we are trying to make a point. We sometimes end up screaming at each other, but we know that it is because of how much we care. It would be terrible if we did not communicate and are indifferent to each other all the time. I feel that it is through these highly charged discussions that we learn to understand each other more and grow in love. Nonetheless, I suppose we must work towards having more subdued discussions. Hopefully, I will mellow, and you mature with age. But never stop talking to Mummy, okay? You can tell me anything and know that I will always be here to walk you through life's ups and downs.

You may think that everything that is written in this letter you already know. That may be true, but these things are what I think are most important for you to remember as you reach the milestone of turning 21.

Hereon, I have to let you go and allow you to grow on your own. I pray for God's protection over you every day, that He will not let you go.

Loving you always,
Mummy

JANET GOH is the manager and director of a trading company for scrap materials. Armed with a degree in Civil Engineering, she joined her family business 25 years ago, trading primarily in recovered paper and scrap plastics with partners in USA, Europe, Japan and Singapore to manufacturers in Southeast Asia. Mother to three adult children, Janet values her time with them and believes in open communication at all times.

Janet and her daughter Rachel.

Face Your Future Bravely

Jenny Wee

Dear Ashley

Mummy loves you very much.

I know that growing up is not easy. It has never been easy. So many choices and decisions. So many possibilities and doubts. So many distractions! Very often, we are strangers in this world at different stages of our lives. I experienced so much growing pains when I was your age. It took me many years to learn that I do not have to run into a crashing storm every single time I think about dancing in the rain. Mummy wants you to know that; and to learn better.

When I was a child, I had a single-minded determination to do well in all the tasks I was given. When Grandma asked me to sweep and mop the floor, I would do it and make sure that the entire floor was squeaky clean. Mind you, your Grandma's house was a huge property with a garden and pond.

While the rest of your uncles and aunties were riding bicycles, screaming with laughter and catching insects,

I was a very serious child. I understood the importance of responsibility very well from a young age, and I understood that it was important to do my part for the family being the eldest daughter.

But this does not mean that Mummy is a block of wood. To be honest, I love my childhood and have many fond memories too.

I had a culture shock when I was enrolled in school. My classmates did not have to do any housework and they had so many toys to play with. They went on holidays and everything in their lives looked so nice and picture perfect. While I envied them secretly, I accepted a simple truth: everyone is different and every family is different.

I love my Dad and Mum, and I love my family. My parents are practical people and we lead a no-frills lifestyle. We may not have an easy, carefree life but we are a family, and as a family we will stick together through thick and thin.

I was competitive in school because national examinations are what levels the playing field for everyone in Singapore. It did not matter if I had the luxury of going on a European holiday during the school break, or if I had that fancy pencil box and matching school bag to bring to school. We studied the same syllabus in school. We had the same teachers in class. We went through the same examinations. Public examinations make everyone equal. I did not have the luxury of tuition but I compensated by sheer hard work and unquestionable diligence. School became a place where I could shine and find my purpose. I worked very hard; I studied while my friends were out partying and having fun.

I first heard the word "meritocracy" from one of my

primary school teachers. It became my de facto mantra in life. I do not think I am pretty; there are many prettier and more fun-loving girls out there. Maybe I don't understand the appeal of popularity and fun. I refuse to let society's definition of "pretty" define my station and success in life. To do well, I do not have to be the prettiest and I do not have to be the most popular girl in school. Against all odds and defying everyone's expectations, I made it through university. I graduated with First Class Honours in Microbiology and I was consistently on the Dean's list every school term.

I took up the Biotechnology course because it was logical. I was the type of student that excelled in any subject because I was attentive in class and I was hardworking. But my decision was largely influenced by my Dad. He told me that Singapore is at a stage of nation-building that will require technical professionals that can advance the country in specific technical fields. He said that biotechnology as going to be one of the most in-demand courses in a booming industry.

My Dad was not wrong. But there were two things he did not consider. Firstly, all industries will follow a cyclical path and new technology will take over and new fads will arise as needs change. Secondly, he did not consider my dreams. Not once did he ask me what I wished to study or to become. But it is the way parenthood was conducted during my growing up years. We were brought up believing that our parents knew best, and very often, they really did. As a child, with little adult understanding of the world, I naturally depended on my parents for guidance.

Looking back, I wished I could have been exposed to a wider range of experiences. There was no Google or social media then. I wish there had been such things as five-minute craft videos to help me learn things quickly! Radio, local television and newspapers connected us to the outside world. Dad worked as a photo editor for *The Straits Times* and he travelled the world for work. All of us love to gather with him at the dining table whenever he was home, to listen to his colourful stories and glean life lessons. Because of that, if my Dad formed an opinion, that opinion stuck in my mind.

I wish I could have pursued a course in business and finance. I am sure I would have done well because I am intelligent, dilligent and hardworking. I have a sharp and critical mind. But I was never given the confidence to pursue, nor exposed to the possibility. Secretly, I harboured thoughts of being a corporate eagle and a head honcho. I can visualise being a part of a multinational corporation, chairing multi-discipline task force and managing the regional business. My life would have been very different!

This is why when it comes to you, dear Ashley, I am most determined to expose you to as many things and possibilities as possible. Contrary to popular opinion, I am not a crazy Tiger Mom. From ballet, to baking and painting classes—even aikido—Mummy wants you to try everything and to experience as much of life as humanly possible. How do you know you can be a good doctor? Or a lawyer? Or even a politician one day? Or maybe you prefer to work in a museum as a curator or to teach in a university? Perhaps you wish to be a business executive in an international corporation? Or owner of a new start-up? Would being a social worker or a counsellor appeal to you instead?

The possibilities in front of you and available to you are endless, Ashley.

Honestly, Mummy does not have the full answer to everything in life. However, I know that your life is just starting. The chapters are still unfolding and your story is only beginning. It fills me with so much pride that you are doing well in secondary school. I see you putting hard work into your studies and displaying that sheer grit and determination to do well in school.

But above all, you step up to take care of your younger brother when Mummy is busy with work. I see so many elements of myself in you. No matter what, we need to challenge ourselves more and learn new things at every stage of our lives. Learning is dynamic and must not cease. There is a whole new world in front of you. New technologies to make learning better, more immersive and a lot more fun. I want you to be able to take advantage of all these tools in front of you to develop, grow and find your own unique value in this rapidly-changing world.

When I made it to the Dean's List back in university and earned a First Class Honours, many foreign universities flocked to offer me exemptions and scholarships to pursue my PhD in research. I could pick from elite institutions in Australia, United Kingdom and America. There was even an offer from Germany! It was all very flattering but I was afraid and was also overwhelmed by all the sudden attention. I had so many worries on my mind – what would student life be like overseas? Can I cope with the demands? How do I communicate with my teachers and classmates? Where do I live? Can I afford the rent and expenses? What would happen to my parents and siblings when I am away? I know I will miss them and what if they miss me too? What about my pet puppies? Would I adapt to the food overseas? What if I miss my local chicken rice and spicy curry? Would I be safe overseas? What if I fall sick? Is the drinking water as safe as that in Singapore? You may laugh at my worries, Ashley, but I assure you, it was all very real and important to me then.

So many questions, so few answers at that young age. It was tough. I was left alone to make all these life-changing decisions at that juncture of my life. I was worried of unforeseen consequences. I was fearful of making mistakes, of change. No one was advising me. My Dad was busy working and travelling; my Mum was kept busy with the family business and caring for the family. I couldn't bear to cause my parents any more stress—I didn't want to be a burden. If I had taken that overseas scholarship, I would have led a very different life. I would have seen a wider, broader spectrum of life. It would have moulded my character development differently. Who knows?

Follow your dreams, Ashley, and try new adventures! However, do not follow blindly or be ill-prepared. Be inquisitive and be brave. But always exercise caution and care.

This is why Mummy brought you to see the terracotta warriors in the tomb of the Qin Emperor. I want you to see the vibrancy of history and culture and to open your eyes to the colours and diversity of human civilisation. Do you recall how we climbed up Mount Emei? We did it to witness the majestic natural wonders in the best way possible: being there in person and together! So many books, tales and movie dramas have tried to capture it but nothing beats witnessing it with our own eyes and absorbing the beauty of the place.

There will be time one day to visit London Bridge and to see the Eiffel Tower. But sights like Mount Emei in China and visiting the panda sanctuaries and historical places in Chengdu, these are priceless life experiences. When we climbed Mount Emei together, it was to show you that despite the cold blasts of winter, we can do it together if we are aligned and we build confidence through proper and in-depth trip research. These are the learning points I wish to impart to you.

Overcoming challenges in life is like climbing a mountain. It looks insurmountable on first impression; very often we get intimidated and endless questions fill our minds. We give the inner fear and self-doubts more credit than necessary. We cannot let such fears trap us. Mummy could have done and achieved much more if there was someone there when I was growing up to talk to and counsel me. To be very honest, Ashley, there is really no such thing as a "life template". What we need in life is simply a loving and caring voice and counsel to work through these fears and doubts and a sense of self-driven purpose to progress and to get things done.

It is important to learn to be still and listen to everything without prejudice. Be calm and open-minded to new knowledge and new techniques as well as new ideas and new possibilities. Be patient with results and know that Mummy is always here to discuss, support and work things out with you every waking step of my life. I wished I could learn to be still and listen to my inner dreams when I was younger; and be braver when faced with uncertainties and doubts. I took the road of least resistance but that is not always ideal. I read recently that when everything is uncertain, everything that is important becomes clearer.

What I have missed out in my growing years, I do not wish that on you, my dearest Ashley. Mummy wants to do things with you while I am still healthy and well. I want to watch you grow; and hopefully, we can create more wonderful memories together and that you will cherish my efforts.

There is an old song that Mummy secretly loved when I was in school. It does not sound anything like Justin Bieber or Selena Gomez or The Chainsmokers, but it was hip during my time. The song by Johnny Mathis is titled *Life Is A Song Worth Singing*.

> Life is a song worth singing
> Why don't you sing it
> You hold the key in the palm of your hand - use it
> Don't blame your life on the master plan - change it
> Only you generate the power to decide what to do
>   with your life
> You're a fool if you think you're helpless!
> You control what you do with your life

You are a blessing to everyone around you, Ashley. Mummy knows this for a fact. Watching you grow up and develop yourself is my great privilege. Face your future bravely. I am so proud of you, Ashley. You will shine!

Loving you to bits,
Mummy

JENNY WEE is the owner of an aesthetic business chain and a consultant for a F&B lifestyle group spearheading many regional projects. She graduated with First Class Honours in Microbiology and a Post-graduate diploma in Education. Her journey into entrepreneurship started when she launched a successful online parenting forum and founded a business distributing baby products.

Jenny is also an active community leader: she is a District Councillor with South West Development Council (SWCDC) where she is the Vice-Chairperson of the Family and Resilience Functional Committee. During her service at SWCDC, she has helmed projects such as Weworkz and the Baby Bliss programme, both implemented at district level. Jenny was presented a Public Service medal at the National Day Awards 2017. She is also a member of the School Advisory Committee for Radin Mas Primary School. Jenny enjoys travelling and cooking for her family. She is also an avid gardener and an advocate for sustainability.

Jenny and Ashley at Mount Emei.

A Letter To My Daughter Going Away To University

Sangeeta Mulchand

My dear Nicola,

It's finally time. You've done your rounds, said your goodbyes, packed your bags, and are ready to hop out of our family nest and stretch your wings.

It's normal to feel nervous, even a little scared. Because we've moved around a lot, our family is our village. We've said goodbye to others, but until now, never to each other. At least not for any length of time. And yet, here you are, my beautiful, smart, ambitious daughter, with a brilliant IB diploma in one hand and admission to medical school in the other, one foot out of the nest and raring to go... but that other foot keeps sticking, doesn't it?

So, is this it then? Once that foot comes unstuck, will you be on your own?

The short answer is No. You will never really be on your own. You see, Nicola, whether you are 5 or 50, here or 10,516 kilometres away, I am still your mother, and there is an invisible umbilical cord connecting us, which I will yank periodically to remind you who you belong to.

I'll nag you about grades and those twice-yearly dental visits. Those care packages that parents send to their kids to make sure they know they are missed? Expect them. Of course things will change—but only in good ways. Think of it this way: until now, we have been your supervisors—from here, we will be your consultants.

But before we get to that part, just a few final pieces of advice. I know you probably don't need it, but it's in my job description, so bear with me.

Going to university—and snagging a coveted spot in the medical faculty—is an incredible opportunity. All those dreams in the air are now within reach. Keep them in sight and don't stop working toward them. In a new city, with new friends, new experiences and newfound freedom, it can be easy to get distracted. Remember how hard you've worked to earn this privilege, and keep your eye on the ball.

Show up on time, every time. Come prepared. Listen. Ask questions. Participate. University is not about consensus and correct answers. Read beyond the syllabus and look for different opinions, look at their justifications and arguments. Discuss, agree or disagree, it doesn't matter which. But enjoy the intellectual dances. Remember that you need those grades to get into your second year—and beyond—so work hard. But you're not only there for the grades. You are there to be educated and to pursue a passion, so don't forget to do that too. And at the end of your journey, you will have the tools to shape and change this world of ours in wonderful and amazing ways, ways that will make it into something better than it is today. And that is a rare and unique opportunity.

So Nicola, make academics your priority.

Outside university, build a network. Make friends with those who are equally excited to be there, equally fascinated by the possibilities, and push each other to grow. People who are comfortable with themselves will offer you friendship that is honest. Those who are hardworking and serious about building their futures will motivate you to be disciplined and dedicated to achieving your own. And those who can laugh at themselves? This lot will keep you sane. You're already good at this, with networks spanning four cities. What you haven't had to do—so far—is to create a network that also keeps you safe. Have a buddy system in place after dark. Always arrive and leave a party, a pub or any other place with a friend or a group of friends. If you have no one to cycle home with at night, plan to stay over with someone you know well. Or take a taxi home. If, despite this, you find yourself in a bad situation and cannot get out of it, fight back. You know the drill. Keep your thumb outside your fist when throwing a punch, and put your whole body weight behind it. Remember that reporting someone makes them less likely to try again. Keeping yourself safe is one thing you should never compromise on. Besides, it much more fun when you have someone to travel with.

Related topic: If something doesn't feel right, don't do it. It's fine for people to invite you to join them. But you can always say no, however hard that may sometimes be. Many people are afraid that if they say no, they may not be invited again, or perhaps that others will think less of them. But don't do anything you are not 100 per cent confident about. There are some things that cannot be fixed if they are lost: your life, your health, your reputation. Trust your instincts, even if you cannot explain them. If it does not feel right, don't. Remember, you've been practicing saying No since you were 2 years old. In three languages. You've got this!

I'm going to sneak in a word about boys here (I heard that eyeroll!), and this also relates to your safety. I'll keep it short, I promise. If it's a first date, go somewhere that is fairly busy, and tell at least one person—preferably someone who won't think it's a good idea to "drop by"—where you'll be and who you are with. Meet for drinks rather than dinner, so if it doesn't work out, you can get out with minimum fuss. If he turns out okay, be yourself. If he's not going to like you for who you are, then it is better not have wasted your time. That said, if you decide you don't like him, let him down gently. It will make other boys much more confident about asking you out.

Dating is like shoe shopping. You try on a pair you think you might like, and walk around in them for a bit to see how comfortably they fit. If they're uncomfortable now, they will only become more uncomfortable later. Try on another pair. If these feel okay, have them wrapped up and take them out of the shop. But this doesn't mean you can't decide at some point that you prefer a different pair. This works both ways, and along the way, you'll figure out what you like and what you don't. But also know your deal breakers: if he puts you down, is abusive, jealous, or tells you what you can or cannot do or wear. Here's another one: if he doesn't like your friends, or your friends don't like him, stop and reevaluate. And if he decides to break up with you, do not stalk him on Facebook/Instagram/Snapchat or whatever the latest platform may be. It's depressing and won't change a thing. Get some of that triple chocolate fudge ice cream and have a good cry. Then move on. Perhaps you will get together again at some point in the future—in the meantime, there may be some pretty cool boots in the next shop.

Talking about shops, let's quickly revisit money and bank accounts. The thing about them is that once they are empty, they usually stay that way. So have a budget and stick to it. The trick is to stinge at the beginning of the month, and splurge at the end of it so the money is replenished in time for you to fill your fridge again. Learn to stretch your budget to cover all your necessities—your room, food, laundry, toiletries, stationery—as well as the fun stuff—eating out, going to the movies, the gym or the pub, birthday presents for your friends, the whole lot. There will also be other expenses, things you never even considered, so always put something aside.

We are your safety net in a real emergency, but true independence means creating your own safety net. So keep a close eye on where your money's going. Also on money, there are few things that will destroy friendships and your reputation more than borrowing money. Don't borrow, and avoid lending unless it's a good friend and a genuine emergency. People who borrow casually are likely to do so again. And again. Avoid them, and make sure you don't become them. We've made enough jokes about "adulting". But you will be held accountable for your actions. You may get to make your own rules, but remember that they are there, especially because many of the situations that you will now encounter will entail making decisions that may have consequences. And sometimes, there may not be a second chance.

Getting into a car with a drunk driver just once, is one time too many.

Having unprotected sex just once, is one time too many.

Crossing the road while looking at just one message, is one message too many.

Leaving your bike unlocked just one night, is one night too many.

In every case, it seems like the sort of thing that would never happen to you. Until it does. And when things go wrong, they can go very, very wrong. In the best case scenario, it will cost you money, in the worst case, it could destroy your life. Or someone else's. Actions have consequences. No matter how tempting, there are certain lines that should never be crossed. Know what those lines are for you. They are the same ones you would draw for your sisters.

I know you're smart about drugs and I am confident that you will stay away from them. But let's just put this down. The attitude in some parts of the world, and in university, may be much more liberal, in particular about soft drugs. There could be some pressure on you to fit in—maybe "just one drag, it won't hurt".

Don't let yourself be pressured—or ridiculed—into doing anything you don't want to. Someone might try to goad you into proving that you're not a wimp or that you're cool enough to be part of their group. Needing drugs to be cool makes you quite the opposite. I know you will avoid this just because. That's the best attitude to take. Also keep in mind that just because someone says something is safe, it doesn't mean that it is—many young adults are no longer around to tell the tale. You don't need to explain or defend your stand, this just leaves the door open for argument. Say no and change the subject. Better still, walk away.

Nicola, as time passes, you will find that some things will change, and other things will stay the same. You will be at university, have a room of your own, make new friends, and begin working towards the career of your dreams. But you will still have your home with us, a family that will continue to drive you crazy, the friends you have made in the last years, your music, and all the small and big things that make you you.

Sangeeta and her daughter Nicola.

When you leave, the empty space that you leave here will be saved for when you come home, because it is a space that is perfectly and uniquely yours. But you will also make new spaces in the places you are headed to. I remember how your heart broke when we left Holland and all things familiar five years ago. Yet, you've had an amazing—and an amazingly full—five years here. And now it is here that is hard to leave. But you've done this enough times to know that what is the end of something is also the beginning of something new. And knowing you, it will be something pretty awesome.

So lift that foot, get going—there is a whole world waiting to be conquered by the whirlwind that is you. Don't forget why you're there—if a little guilt helps, remember that we have worked hard to provide you with this opportunity.

Also remember that I love you very much, so let me hear from you often. You don't have to call every day. In fact, I hope that it will be so incredible that you won't have time to. But WhatsApp, Snapchat, email every once in a while so I can keep up with your adventures, and remind you how much you are loved and missed.

With love,
Mama

SANGEETA MULCHAND has more than three decades of journalism and editing experience under her belt, in cities from Tokyo to Amsterdam. She cut her teeth with Singapore's largest news organisation, Singapore Press Holdings, as a journalist for the *Business Times,* and from there, built her career in the cities that her husband's diplomatic career took their young family to. She's had the opportunity to do an amazing breadth of work, from editing for Dow Jones Newswires in Tokyo and being Benelux correspondent for *Screen International* to writing for *World Press Photo*, and now, as Managing Editor of *Word of Art* in Singapore. Yet her proudest achievements are her three daughters, brought up through trial and according to her, probably too many errors, but through the eyes of a mother, incredible human beings with a drive to make a difference.

A Mother's Emotional Odyssey

Zalina Gazali

Dearest Bubba,

Nineteen years ago, you stole my heart, robbed me of sleep and hijacked my rest. And was guilty as charged for defining "happy" for me.

From your first cry at three in the morning after the eight hours of labor (or was it 12? I forgot everything as soon as you were in my arms), I knew that life as I had known would cease to exist. I knew that life would be more joyous, more amazing, more wonderful, more incredible. But I also knew that life would be so much more frightening.

Not because there was anything wrong with you. You were, still are, and always will be perfect in my eyes. (Cue: "Awwww!") I say "frightening" because the second we locked eyes, I no longer was one self. I no longer was responsible for just me. I now had an extension of me, whom I had to be answerable for, whom I instantly wanted to guard and protect with every ounce of my being.

And that scared the beeswax out of me.

You would think that now, almost two decades later, with you off to university, nearly out of your teens and dipping your toe into young adulthood, I would already have kicked and pummeled Fear into its rightful place. But noooo. Not even close. In fact, Fear has teamed up with that thing called Anxiety. And when these two tag-team, they make a white-knuckled rollercoaster ride look like a stroll in the park while eating ice cream covered with rainbow sprinkles. In slow-motion.

In short, yes, your Mama is scared. Because the world is a scary place and because I do not want you to be scared. I know my logic sounds warped. Welcome to the chapter in *The Book Of Mom* titled "Mama Does Not Have All The Answers".

I hope this does not disappoint you. You were always inquisitive, even as a child. For every "Why, Mama?" that I answered, another eight would follow. When you were 5, my answering "Why is the sky blue?" could well end up in an explanation of how to milk a cow. I loved how I could fill you with knowledge and trivia, and you would hang on to my every word, eyes wide like plates. Your innocent curiosity about everything was endearing, and your contemplative nature adorable. It was not surprising then that you grew up to have an inquiring mind, and the passion to match it. It also did not come as a surprise that you became a very caring, considerate and thoughtful young lady.

Now, my responses to your "Why, Mama?" can no longer be simple. Where once I could reply easily and maybe even make up an answer, I sometimes now am taken aback at your very question itself. The issues you are concerned about now are deeper, and your own take on these matters so much more profound. I am both in awe and trepidation at how much you care about the world. Sometimes, to be honest, I feel you care too much.

Don't get me wrong. I am glad to see you take an interest in serious issues affecting the world. I love your confidence in not shying away from verbal discourse on these issues, even if things between us get heated. It shows me that you are strong-minded, you're not superficial and there is desire in you to want to make the world a better place. It makes me mad proud that your heart is in the right place. What troubles me is that some of these issues are so dark and serious, and there are no straightforward answers.

When you share your concerns about gender equality, majority privilege, poverty, crime, human trafficking and the like, I know that I can no longer pretend that I can keep you safely in a bubble. Also I don't want to keep you in a state of ignorant bliss. And I certainly don't ever want you to "lower" your voice. So I will say this: if you believe in the good that your speaking up can do, don't let people convince you that you're wrong. Instead, prove to them that you're right. Because these issues are real. More real than all 17 seasons of *Keeping Up With The Kardashians* put together. These issues warrant attention and action.

Just be mindful to not let the problems of this Big, Bad World affect you to the point where Fear and Anxiety hijack your heart. My own heart breaks a little when I see you sometimes cry at injustices because you feel so much for a cause. I hate that I cannot stop you from feeling pain. But I recognise you have to go through all the feelings, good and bad.

Having said that, our conversations now are a lot more interesting and thought-provoking. I love that we bounce views and hear out each other's perspectives.

My Mama role is thus always expanding. Beyond protecting you, I want to gently steer you in the right direction emotionally, so that you will not be overwhelmed. To help without interfering, to guide without pushing. But it's a constant dance, learning how to not push too far or pull back too much. Ultimately, you will have to make you own decisions, directions and choices. All I can do is to inject optimism and inspiration where I can.

The world may not be all unicorns and rainbows (and I hear that mermaids may not be real, dang it).

Yes there are problems, but there are also solutions. When you take steps to heal the world, that will give you a sense of happiness and contentment. The journey that your passion takes you will pave the way for experiences that no textbook can teach you.

Speaking of textbooks, let me speak about another huge leap that you are about to take. I am so darn proud of you that you will headed for an institute of higher learning. All that hard work has paid off—it was all you. I helped, of course, offering to bring you snacks when you were stressed out studying. You're welcome. Your new passage will not only give you vast knowledge, but it will be an internship of sorts in the School of Life. Exciting times are ahead, Bubba. And more snacks, this I promise you.

I sense that while you are eager and enthused to start this new chapter in your life, you are also nervous. That is understandable as you will be starting afresh, having to make new friends and adjusting to life on campus. But these experiences are as thrilling as they are nerve-wrecking. So turn that hesitant smile into a gleeful one.

Sure, we butted heads on which would be the best path for you to take, the biggest disagreement being whether you should study abroad, or stay where your Mama can give you a hug without having to hop on a plane.

I never thought the Empty Nest Syndrome would hit me, but it did, and it hit hard. At first, I did not understand why I was so sad at the thought of you going away. The thought of you leaving gave me such a hollow, empty feeling that reached the pit of my stomach. I also felt guilty that I was not happy for you to be able to spread your wings and soar. Why was I feeling like this when as your Mom, I should be wanting nothing but everything for you. Then it dawned on me: I was terrified. Terrified that your leaving meant you would outgrow me, maybe not dramatically, but in a barely noticeable, quietly subtle, inevitable growing up sort of way.

I imagined us having a tearful goodbye at the airport, and me coming home and wandering around aimlessly in your empty room, and hugging your soft toys, weeping yet more tears to the soundtrack of imaginary violins. I imagined us trying to stay connected and the daily calls become every-other-day calls, then weekly, then as and when...

Fact: You're the exclamation mark in the happiest sentence that I could ever possibly write. Thus I was petrified that you would not need me anymore. You see, my little one, your capacity to fill me with delight is matched by your capacity to fill me with dread.

Apart from these sentiments, I also wanted to make sure you would be making an informed decision about university. I did not want to take an authoritative stance but I wanted the decision-making process to be a consultative one, seeing how this is your life. As your Mom, I always want to be the enabler for all your hopes and dreams. The equation is pretty simple. You Happy = Happy Me. But sometimes difficult decisions have to be made, for longer term benefits, True, part of me wanted to selfishly keep you near home, because I was not ready to cut the symbolic umbilical cord. I'll be fully ready when you're 55. Maybe. However, part of me also felt it was not the right time for you to fly off on your own. Hence, I am thankful and grateful that you were able to understand and accept the rationale behind the benefits of you staying in Singapore.

I know you are still a little disappointed that the overseas experience won't be yours for now. But I am really proud at your sensibility at being able to see the advantages of a locally-based education, and that you will, God-willing, still be able to have an international exposure in time to come.

I'm relieved that you are now looking forward to this next step, because I want you to enjoy it. I get caught up in your excitement when you ask "Mama, can I get a lava lamp for my new dorm room? Oh, and a beanbag?" It is surreal that my little baby is not so little anymore and will be living apart from me for a bit. You seemed to have gone from 9 months to 19 years faster than I could say "Iman, clean your room!" (I will miss you replying "Itsnotthatmessymooooom!")

You will enjoy this new phase in your life, the learning, the activities, the camaraderie, and, okay, the meeting of boys.

(Breathe, Mama, breathe). It is to be expected, I guess. Your Papa and I began a serious relationship when we were in uni. So I have to be prepared that you may meet the love of your life soon.

To quote Shakespeare, "Love is a many splendored thing". Beyoncé sang 'For there's only love. And this sweet, sweet love. After all is said and done'. So yes, my love, I want you to find love and be in love. I hope you will one day find someone wonderful, because you have so much love to give, and are so worthy of so much love. Don't be afraid to fall in love—head over heels while you're at it. I hope you will have the full stars-in-eyes, heart-melting moments with that someone special, and that you will be treated with adoration and tenderness that you deserve.

Take your time, though, Bubba. There really is no deadline for when to fall in love. Worry not about when to start looking or what is a good "coupledom" age. You will find each other when the time is right. Let me jump in with a little story. Your Papa and I met when we were 15 and became good friends over many years. It was only almost a decade later that the courtship actually started, and this was strengthened because we had a strong foundation of friendship. So don't underestimate the importance of not only loving your partner, but also being each other's cheerleader and supporter. Never feel that you cannot share your innermost thoughts with your significant other, because if you both are truly in sync, there is nothing that a heart-to-heart cannot overcome.

That said, you do not need anyone to complete you—you are more than enough on your own. Accept nothing less than what you would give to yourself, and at no point should you ever let anyone disrespect you or tell you that you are not worthy. Promise me that. What they tell you matters only if you believe it. Your self-worth and self-love is fundamental. Love yourself first, and everything else will follow.

I know you sometimes worry about failing in relationships, especially since your Papa and I are now just best friends without wedding rings on our fingers. But don't let whatever missteps your parents have made define you, and don't let them deter you. You are you, and you will make your own magic happen.

One question you frequently ask me is, "Mama, will everything be okay?" Each time, I pause, and remember Doris Day's syrupy strains:

Que sera, sera
Whatever will be, will be
The future's not ours to see
Que sera, sera
What will be, will be....

Essentially, this still holds true. There is certainly the element of chance and destiny at play. But you have the choice to do what you want to do, and to be who you want to be.

So to your recurring question, my answer will always be, "Yes, my sweetheart. It will all be okay. Even when things are not okay."

Remember that you're allowed to sometimes not do well in things. You're allowed to trip and fall, to be in situations you do not like, and to have days where you just cannot do anything more that curl up on the sofa and listen to sad songs.

As long as you don't give up and find a way to pick yourself up and try, and try again. You have the power over your actions, thoughts, feelings, and over your happiness. So, please, choose to be happy.

I treasure each and every memory we have together. Even the times you accidentally left a Lego on the floor for me to step on. And I am excited for the new memories we'll be making. Especially the ones involving you cleaning your room without me asking you 305 times.

Thank you for showing me what loyalty looks like, what love is capable of, and how to put on eyeshadow that does not make me look like I was punched in the face. Know that no matter how much I say I love you, I always love you more than that. You may have outgrown being carried in my arms, but you will never outgrow my hugs and my heart.

My dearest Iman, you are on the way to becoming an accomplished and amazing woman. So keep the faith, especially when you take any leaps. Don't let your fears and anxiety stop you from reaching out for your dreams. Do what needs to be done to bring on happiness: sing, dance, save the world, eat breakfast for dinner, watch the whole season of a series in a day...

Be full of joy. Carpe the heck out of the diem. And my darling girl, live exuberantly.

Love ya, my Bubba,
Your Mama

ZALINA GAZALI is Mama to a 19 year-old daughter, and subscribes to the parenting approach that love and respect is enriched with friendship and fun. An alumna of the National University of Singapore with an Honour's Degree in Sociology, she has worked in both public and private sectors, and is currently a manager with an asset management company. Zalina is an advocate of work-life balance and enjoys travelling, dance fitness and things that give happy vibes. Her outlook on life is founded on sound sensibility, elevated by the power of possibility. She hopes as she leads by example, her daughter will live life with confidence, zeal, passion, joy and most of all, kindness.

Zalina (left) and daughter Iman (right).

The Importance Of Identity & A Good Red Lipstick

Cynthia Chew

To my beloved Solana,

My firstborn, my sunshine. As you are part Filipino with some Spanish influence, we wanted a Spanish name for you. When we came across the name "Solana", which means sunshine, in Spanish, we knew right away that that would be your name. Life has never been the same since and is so much brighter because of you.

Here's your story.

Unlike you, who at 17 can tell me that you want to have children (even adopt them if you can), I haven't always wanted to be a mother. The idea only started brewing after I got married. When I was finally ready to have a child, it took a year of trying to conceive before you finally happened. You certainly added spice into my life. When I was pregnant with you, I was often craving for peppery food so I would often douse my fish soup or yong tau foo with lots of white pepper. Perhaps a little too much—as you were also known as the "hiccup baby". The experience of a life growing inside me is truly an amazing one—but you couldn't wait to see the world.

I remember the afternoon when you arrived. I was ready to go for a work photoshoot but the contractions started to kick in. Thinking they were just Braxton-Hicks, I checked into the hospital, assuring my colleagues that I would be back later. Who knew that you were ready to make us parents that day! And that's how you were born, three-and-a-half-weeks earlier than the estimated delivery date. As I cradled you in my arms, I was partly in shock but mostly in awe of you.

The first great pang of sadness came when we were told that you had a congenital disorder (which was later corrected with surgery), and felt another wave of sadness when you couldn't come home with me due to jaundice. Nobody warned me about the number of times my heart would plunge and soar on this great big rollercoaster ride called parenthood.

I have enjoyed watching you grow, from that super shy and timid girl who is always afraid of speaking up in public, to a young woman who has slowly but surely found her voice and confidence. Your quietude is also what builds your keen sense of observation. But being timid has also made you an easy target and a victim of bullying in school. My instinct as a mother to protect you and to find justice kicked in. But I also knew it was important to take a step back and let you deal with it. I still marvel at how you endured the entire ordeal without crying or getting mad—okay, perhaps you teared a little when relating the incidents to me. You remained stoic in the face of adversity. I am so proud of you.

As the daughter of a former beauty editor of 20 years, you had an early sneak into the wonderful world of cosmetics and all things related to beauty. I'm proud that you picked up makeup skills on your own—from Youtube rather than me, but that's okay. Who hasn't picked up a new skill from YouTube? It's good to see how you discover things on your own, experiment, and keep practising. When it comes to creativity or making your own statement, I'd rather you own it, and not be influenced by anyone, not even me.

While you may prefer nude lipsticks now, I hope that you'll eventually find a penchant for red lipsticks as I have. Let me share this one little secret about the red lipstick. While some may beg to differ by saying that the eyeliner or mascara or even the foundation is the one makeup item that will change your look, nothing beats a pair of red lips when you want to make the ultimate beauty statement. It is bold, it is loud, and it takes lots of confidence to put it on, but it is the OG game changer. So I hope that you will find the audacity to wear a red lipstick one day.

I'm happy that we are sharing more similarities now than before. We enjoy simple activities like working on Word Search and colouring, and we have the same colour preference and sense of style. Regardless of what you choose to put on, be comfortable in your own skin, be body confident and have a love for life without being excessive.

I know how you feel about your body. But do you know, I wish I had your body when I was growing up? I would have loved to have had bigger boobs, more curves, and more flesh than just "skin and bones" as people often used to say about me. Contrary to the popular perception of beauty, I hated being underweight because I often got teased, or even called names. The fact is, you have the better half of the Filipino genes. But what matters is not the size but your health. God has blessed you with a healthy and able body so take good care of it and stay healthy! Your health is definitely more important than your grades.

Want to know what else is more important than your studies? Your faith. Yes, it is far more important than trying to achieve A's in school. School hasn't been easy for you. I want you to know that every disappointment that you have experienced—each time you called to tell me that you didn't pass, that you have improved, or how hard you've tried, I have felt it with you. As your mother, I shared fully in your disappointment, and it saddened me that my child didn't get a chance to experience the pride and joy of getting good grades.

The education system and path in Singapore isn't very kind to late bloomers or people who are not all that academically driven. I tried to provide all the help you needed but still, with a heavy heart, I watched you struggle over the years, wondering how you would catch up.

But I know that the day you got your PSLE results is one you will cherish for the rest of your life. You broke down when you saw that you had passed all your subjects—even mathematics.

I was excited when you first shared your plan to follow in my footsteps and to go into journalism. However, things didn't quite turn out the way we wanted. You are now pursuing a Diploma in Community Care and Social Service instead, and you speak so passionately about working with children in the future. Talk about an unexpected turn of events—and such a noble call. I dare say that this is the road God has paved out for you—all the other doors leading to journalism were closed in your post-secondary study considerations and course applications.

Today, you have blossomed to become someone far more than I could ever imagine. When you were just a baby, your Lola (Filipino for grandma) used to say "she has a good heart". How did she know that? Truly, I am now a witness of how much goodness there is in you. Your demure and gentle nature, never breaking any rules (even when you were still little, you would point to the "No Outside Food Or Drinks" sign at an eatery when we brought out your baby food and drinks), always ready to give in even when you don't want to (especially with your sister) and your show of tender loving care towards animals, are all tantamount to the love of God in you.

As God has made me stewards of you and your sister, I had better not mess this up. I will do my best to bring you girls up as morally and spiritually right as possible. As Christians, know that our faith is a gift from God and it is far more precious and important than academia or any scholarly pursuits. I don't care if you never become rich or famous; a successful lawyer or director of a company. What will make me happier is to see you become someone who's compassionate, kind, gentle, helpful and loving.

Go forth and be happy and continue to be everyone's sunshine!

Love,
Mum

* * *

My darling Mila,

You are our little miracle. That's what your name "Mila" means—it is short for Milagros or Miracles in Spanish. Truth is, I was planning on stopping at one child. It was scary to think of going through the process of childbirth again, the night feeds, being sleep deprived and still having to look after a baby while handling a toddler. However, both your father and I each have more than two siblings, so we know what joys—as well as pain—come with sharing life with one another.

The moment we decided to have another child, you happened. The second time does not make it any easier. I had more morning sickness, I was more tired because I had your toddler sister now, I was bigger at the waist, and I carried you all the way to full term—you arrived just one day before the estimated delivery date. We thought we would be more prepared with you, but you came fast and furious that morning. From the moment I was woken up by painful contractions to the bursting of my water bag, to how you were already crowning and all ready to come out before the doctor arrived—it was all so fast!

Going through parenthood a second time meant we were also more "chill" with you. You are quick-witted, an independent learner who is able to pick things up pretty quickly—they say it's the "second-child syndrome" because you have an older sibling to emulate. You started to talk at one, sing at two... the things you used to say would always bring a smile to my face to no end. How proud you made me too. I am often told that you're a carbon copy of me.

Besides the facial features, you also have the same size 0 body shape as I when I was growing up, a knack for being super organised and neat (when you want to be), and you even like the same kinds of music I do: everything from moody tunes to hip hop and rap. Sometimes I think you're too cool for school.

But where we differ is that you're good in art (while I can't draw to save my life), and you excel in sports. I admire the fact that you love to run (I suck at running), that you persevered in ballet even when it became very challenging. You're so good at TikTok, and you're also the fittest of us all in the family.

Over the years, you have wormed your way into Daddy's heart—you've become a daddy's girl. I was a mummy's girl, so I wouldn't know what that is like but I'm sure it's equally endearing. You'd show him affection or share secrets with him. I wish you would share them with me too. And because we're so much alike, I suspect that you might grow up rebellious. I was a rebel myself when I was a teenager so I know full well what's in store for me as your parent, but that doesn't make it any less easier.

Know that I often try to read and understand what is on your mind and heart, and it makes me feel helpless when I am unable to reach deep enough.

Whenever we have a disagreement, I regret having spoken harshly to you. You may think I am unfair to you or even that I'm partial to your sister. I love both of you, but you will discover, when you're a mum yourself (even though right now, you are adamantly against marriage), you will discover that you love your children equally much, but differently.

Such episodes often leave me feeling like I have failed as a mother. But I will not give up. Parenthood doesn't automatically equip me with the right maternal instincts all the time. But I am definitely working on navigating my way through this journey called motherhood.

Mila, we may not share much or talk often but that's why I'm always randomly popping into your room just to have a peak at you and to check on you. I just want you to know that I'm not being weird—it's my way of showing I care and I often hope that you'd invite me in for an update or a chat. I may not understand you now but I'm praying for a breakthrough one day. Just know that I love you.

Let me share what it was like for me as a teenager. I came from a traditional Asian family where parents don't have very open communication with their children and neither do they express their affections openly. As my parents worked most of the times, I was often left to my own devices. So it's true I had a lot of freedom. Yet they were also strict about some things, especially moral values. I was not allowed to wear too-short shorts for example. If I did, I would have to change my attire before I was allowed to leave the house. I also knew that if I ever talked back to them or slam the room door, I would be in big trouble. Respect and piety for our parents were unspoken, but learnt.

As I said previously, I was a rebel at heart. I didn't always tell my parents where I went. One time, I attended a house party and I must have busted my curfew which led them to drive around the estate looking for me. Surprisingly, I didn't get the discipline I deserved. But the incident had left me with all kinds of regret and feeling sorrier than I ever did.

As I reflect on my past, I realise the risk of falling into bad company and ending up in all kinds of trouble. But by some divine intervention, nothing terrible happened. The boys I knew were not total rascals and I knew not to go too far.

You may think I'm not cool or not understanding by not trusting you with boys right now. As cliché as this may sound, it's not so much about you—I just don't trust boys and their adolescent hormones. Ask your Dad about that. The world is also a much scarier place now than it was 30 years ago. We weren't privy to the vast expanse of content that you get from the Internet and social media today. What boys my time were exposed to was probably far more "innocent" in comparison.

Boy-girl relationships are one of the most exhilarating things anyone will ever experience that first crush, first kiss, first boyfriend. You will one day meet boys who will make your heart beat faster and your stomach flutter. You will fall in love, and your heart will also be broken. Perhaps I am just trying to delay the inevitable, but I know I won't be able to protect you forever. That is something everyone will experience at least once in their lifetime—or several times in my case. I am sure your experiences will be different, and they will be uniquely yours. How else are you going to experience the fullness of life, all the pains along with joys? But no matter what happens, know that I will be here for you always.

When I got married in church, I made a vow that I would bring my children up in the Roman Catholic faith and that is exactly what I planned on doing. My hope is for both you and your sister to grow up to be God-fearing and God-loving, to be able to encounter the Lord one day, to experience His love and mercy, to see for yourselves why I love Jesus so much,

Cynthia and her gitls, Solana and Mila.

and for you to love Christ as much as I do. For this, I will never stop praying.

Before I sign off, I want to say thank you to you both, for giving me this great privilege to be your mum. I will never trade it for anything—not even for all the freedom or travel in the world.

Love,
Mum

CYNTHIA CHEW is a mother of two teenage girls and a former beauty editor writing mainly for women's magazines such as *Marie Claire, FEMALE,* and *CLEO.* She first fell in love with writing when she discovered Keats and the Romantics during her post-secondary school studies. Where she used to pen words from journals to poetry, nowadays her writing takes the form of scriptural reflections, often sharing her journey as a firm believer of Christ. This church ministry addict is now a mass communications lecturer at a polytechnic.

Part 4

WISDOM FOR
THE REST OF YOUR LIFE

"Life doesn't come with a manual,
it comes with a mother."
—Unknown

A Letter From Your "Fun" Tiger Mom

Paige Parker

For my dearest daughters, Happy and Bee,

Fabulous, unmapped futures await you both.

Happy, now 17, though brimming with wisdom since youth, you are in the initial phase of early adulthood, with sky-high expectations alongside insecurities and uncertainties galore. For Bee, 12, my wilful, sweetheart child, learning more of yourself and the world, enormous dreams fill your head as the future remains a candy store, bursting with options. As Happy applies to universities, while Bee determines her secondary school path, you both persevere diligently and with purpose, for which I am most proud.

At both of your ages, I knew far less than you two know today. Can you believe I did not even have a passport? Perhaps growing up in American's South, in Rocky Mount, North Carolina (population: 50,000) kept me sheltered from knowing so much so soon. That may sound quaint, but if given a choice, I prefer knowledge and travel—as you have enjoyed—over my small-town, small-minded experience as a youngster. When I did escape, tossed into the madness of university, lost in books and spurred on by mentors, I shed my small-town naivety faster than a popsicle melts on a sizzling summer sidewalk.

At age 26, when I met your father Jim, "for both of us, it had been love at first sight. A *coup de foudre*, as the French say. A lightning bolt", as told in my memoir, *Don't Call Me Mrs Rogers*. Before meeting him, I had dreamed of seeing the world. Then, together, we made it happen by embarking on an adventure that would change me forever: a three-year drive to the ends of the earth and back, circumnavigating the globe, visiting 116 countries.

Undoubtedly, the people from my hometown never could have imagined me battling sand storms, outrunning armed insurgents, confronting corrupt officials, fighting off gropers and grifters, and learning to skilfully deal with malaria, filth and enough red tape to wrap an elephant. But I did. I made it around the world with a Guinness World Record as proof. Others' opinions should never stop you from taking the chance of a lifetime, only to have that experience awaken the woman you were meant to be.

Our decision to leave New York City for Singapore some 13 years ago, was largely for the sake of your futures. Ready for a new adventure, Jim and I uprooted our lives because we believed your lives should embrace Asia, which meant speaking fluent Mandarin and understanding this part of the world. A bit unconventional, yes, but normalcy is often over-rated. Singapore, a melting pot of sorts, gained our favor for obvious reasons: clean air, top-notch health care, excellent schools, sound infrastructure, rule of law, educated population, abundant arts, entertainment and culture, and an exceptional airport.

You are both fortunate to have spent your formative years in Singapore, as part of Nanyang Primary School, where being amongst the smartest in class is cool. I do sometimes agonize that your youths have been stripped with too much studying and tuition, and too little time for riding bikes and dance lessons. Then, I recall that was my childhood. Yours is as third-culture children growing up in Asia, 15,888 kilometers from my birth place. May you never feel as outsiders: not American, not Asian. Third-culture children are famous for belonging everywhere, but nowhere. Still, I imagine your youths in Singapore will help to shape you into resilient, accepting adults.

You have heard me declare, "My job now is to mother. We can be friends when you are grown, perhaps when you are mothers yourselves." Although you have not always liked this, I believe having rules and being the authority as a parent is important as our children are developing. Mothers who befriend their children have a tricky time guiding and disciplining them. Indeed, moms need to push children—only on their strengths, not everything—since most of us are not driven to discover our inherent gifts. We need the extra nudge. We need a mother's special love. I have adored being a "fun" Tiger Mom, as you both call me.

As I consider what's in store for you both, like most mothers, I dream grandly. I want my daughters to be smarter, kinder, prettier, happier, and more successful than I will ever be. Still the truth remains, if you two grow up as contented, thoughtful, productive women, then I have succeeded in my life's most important role. My job has been to build you up, equip you for independence, and encourage you to take off, likely fail, only to fly, or soar, if we all are lucky.

Mothers never know how our children's lives will evolve, where life will lead them. This, indeed, is our risk and reward, a tightrope we walk. My mother and father, I assure you, never imagined I would spend the formative years of their granddaughters' lives on the other side of the planet. Unconditional love allows mothers to give up the reins. We invest in our children's lives because our time with them is our cherished compensation. I hope and pray you both will look back, return to me, and as Bee promises "to always have an extra room available for Mommy".

Through life, I ask each of you to revisit my book *Don't Call Me Mrs. Rogers*, recalling my naivety, struggles, strengths, frustrations and frankness. May the glimpse into my life offer you a nugget of reflection, contemplation, even inspiration. If I can make it around the world, then I know you girls can too, for you are tougher and brighter, ready to go forth with eagerness and curiosity to explore and learn, while fighting for what is right and for what you deserve.

I dream that as adults, you will be part of my returns to places of the world that educated and shaped me. Think of Argentina's majestic Perito Moreno Glacier, India's Calcutta with her crumbling, albeit inspiring aura, and Djenne's massive mud mosque in Mali. May we form new memories together for as long as possible. May we be friends forever.

Please allow me to share a few of life's verities, hopefully planting seeds for you both to go forth to love, work, and play with awareness, albeit on your own terms. All we mothers want is to pave the way for better lives for our children, and for me, in particular, to make sure my daughters have equal and ample choices.

- Say yes to life! Keep your eyes and heart open to all she has to offer.
- Set an example by the way you live.
- Be kind to every single person, no matter their title or income.
- To feed your love of learning, make time to read in both English and Chinese.
- Your bilingualism of fluent Mandarin and English is a gift. Use it.
- As citizens of the world, keep an open mind. Understand both sides of the story, especially when you do not agree.
- Be on time. Hubris is the reason people are late. That is such bad form.
- Arrogance, or knowing it all, breeds ignorance. Travel. Explore. Question. Learn. Listen.
- Speculation is an absolute waste of time. Deal only in substance. Do not gossip. Do not be a fool.
- Never apologize for being ambitious and resourceful.
- Leave home for university. You may always return, but when one leaves, she returns to know home and herself like never before.
- When there is a strong will, there is always a way. Work harder than you think possible on goals and ideals that truly matter. Persist, persist, persevere!
- If you find yourself bogged down, working for something that is not meaningful, then cut yourself some slack. You

are only human. Decide what is important and put your focus there. You cannot be everything to everyone. Learn to prioritize.

- Life is not fair, but please know the world is good. Work to change what you deem immoral and unjust. Understand that baby steps matter: your small acts can accrue to bring transformation.

- You will fail, and that's okay. If possible, fail early in your adult life, since regrouping will be far easier. When you do fail, reflect, learn, perhaps apologize, and move on. Billionaire Oprah Winfrey was fired from her first job as a television anchor. Vera Wang failed to make the 1968 US Olympic figure-skating team, and later was passed over for the top editor's job at *Vogue*. At 40, she started designing wedding dresses, and now at 70, her iconic namesake brand is worth over $600 million.

- Never apologize for saying no. To your boss, your friend, your child, especially the pushy saleswoman at Sephora.

- Do not succumb to the FOMO (Fear of Missing Out) mindset. It never brings peace of mind. Understand someone else will always have more, bigger, better. Be happy for them.

- Stand up for yourself. Always. No one else will, except maybe your mama and daddy, but we cannot do it forever.

- Actions have consequences. You cannot just be along for the ride. Remember your father's goddaughter Grace, killed in a car crash with a drunk driver at the wheel.

- Skip drugs. Even if legal, they dumb you down. Do not drink too much alcohol. For many, drugs and alcohol are a slippery slope to an abyss.

- Never allow men to joke and throw out sexist comments. If a friend, boss, or partner does not respect other women, then he will never respect you. Call him out.
- Dump any guy who tries to control you. Only small, spiteful people want to diminish others.
- Do not follow a guy on his journey. Make him follow you on yours.
- Being a woman can be an advantage in life, business, society, everything. However, using your sexuality to get you places will ruin your sense of self-worth.
- Not understanding money has ruined many marriages, families, and even smart people. Educate yourself.
- Never discuss the cost of things with others, or ask how much someone makes, or how much their car or house costs. Likewise, do not bring up the same about yourself.
- Do not buy every pretty little thing. A prettier one is coming. Plus, sustainability must become our reality. Buy less, but smarter and better. Quality lasts longer, and who knows, may become heirlooms.
- Never forget money is a tool that does not solve all problems. Do not succumb to the singular drive to be rich at all costs. Plenty of rich people are not happy.
- Avoid debt if you can. If starting a business, then perhaps you have no choice, but try to save your money. When you do borrow, pay it back on time, or sooner. Debt is a prison sentence.
- When people laugh at your new ideas, you are probably correct. Plus, you are more likely to succeed, since people pursuing what makes them happy, their passions, are better at what they do. They feel rich, even with a

small bank account.

- When you find a tribe, who respects and inspires you, nurture those bonds. Real friendships are rare and take work.
- Unfortunately, some women will judge you, and maybe even try to break you. Try to ignore them. If not, kill them with kindness, as you pity them.
- Do not put life experiences on hold. Do not put a career path on hold. Do not put children on hold. Do not wait for perfect timing and perfect conditions, which may never arrive.
- When people advise you to relax, tell you there is more time, please know that life is short. Do not wait on the sidelines. Get busy and live with passion, no matter what others say.
- Believing in something bigger than all of us, having faith, can offer life meaning and comfort, especially when you feel lost.
- Your mama might be vain, but I have taught you both that beauty fades, while the brain remains. Never be consumed with your looks, but being consumed with learning is just fine.
- Please do not get tattoos. Ever. Remember removal is painful, tedious, and expensive.
- Take excellent care of your skin. You will pat yourself on the back when you are 50. This means using more sunscreen than you like, far more often than you want.
- Become a fitness addict, enabling you to enjoy more of life's limitless, scrumptious food, which feeds the soul, while increasing your lifespan.

- Learn to cook. "No one is born a great cook. One learns by doing," said Julia Child. You will save money, too.
- Binge-watching Netflix is not a sin. Nor is eating a tub of ice-cream if that's what is needed.

One for the album: Bee, Paige and Happy in Vienna.

- Karma is real. Paying it forward in life, adding more than you take from the world, allows you to sleep well and to know you have done what is right. If you are rotten, then know karma will bite back.
- Trust serendipity. (That's how I met your father!)
- Good manners really do matter.
- You are beautiful exactly as you are. Do not get lost in social media, ads, fads, others' opinions. Know you are just right.
- May you both embrace life, while daring to do the unexpected, with grateful hearts.
- When in doubt, call your mama.

Love you to the moon and back!
Mom, Mama, Mother, Mommy
Paige

PAIGE PARKER moved from New York to Singapore 13 years ago. Paige is a patron, board member and fundraiser for numerous organisations, including the United Women Singapore, Singapore Symphony Orchestra, Asian Civilization Museum, and Singapore Dance Theatre.

Paige, a former advisor to Singapore Fashion Week, enthusiastically supports local fashion, jewellery and art. A graduate gemologist from the Gemological Institute of America, Paige is also a columnist for *The Straits Times,* allowing her a platform to discuss important issues and trends.

At the turn of the millennium, Paige and her husband Jim Rogers spent three years driving around the world, ultimately gaining a Guinness World Record. Paige's best-selling book *Don't Call Me Mrs. Rogers* details the epic circumnavigation, as well as her own personal evolution. Paige is a member of The Explorers Club and Circumnavigator's Club.

Paige and Jim are the proud parents of Happy and Bee. Please connect with Paige on Instagram @iampaigeparker.

The Important Things In Life

Shaan Moledina-Lim

My darling little girl,

This is the hardest letter I have ever had to write. It is the most important one, but also one I hope you will never have to read. Everything that I've written here, I hope to tell you in person… through all the different phases of your life. But, life is wild and unpredictable, and I can't help but have a back-up plan, just in case something were to happen to me before I can tell you everything I need to tell you, and teach you all that I know. And not just things you can learn from the eloquent Maya Angelou, or the inspiring Michelle Obama, but things I've learned as a woman along my journey —life lessons from my stories, from your stories, and all the stories we wrote together.

Music

I take my music very seriously, just like you have ever since you were 4 and could shockingly sing all the lyrics to *We Didn't Start The Fire*. Or the time you were 5 and made a beeline for the deejay booth at an anniversary party to see if you could put in a song request. Then, there was the time you learned the 6 times table by changing the lyrics to Karmin's *Acapella* to the 6 times table. All of that—so me.

So, naturally, this letter has to come with an accompanying soundtrack to listen to while you read this.

- *Racing In The Street* by Bruce Springsteen
- *Wish You Were Here* by Pink Floyd
- *Landslide* by Fleetwood Mac
- *Imagine* by John Lennon
- *All I Want Is You* by U2
- *Blinded By Rainbows* by Rolling Stones
- *Redemption Song* by Bob Marley
- *Man In the Mirror* by Michael Jackson
- *Hymn To Her* by The Pretenders
- *Eres Mi Religión* by Maná

Beauty

Back when you were 2 years old and thought the moon was made of marshmallows and snowflakes, you were invited to your friend Myra's princess-themed tea party. You wore a frou-frou pink dress, your hair pinned up in a bun, secured with a sparkly tiara. You had the best time sipping invisible tea and draping beads and boas all around you, while everyone commented on how pretty the little girls looked all dressed up.

Then, the minute you got home after the party, you stripped off that dress, yanked out the tiara, ran to your box of wooden trains and started playing on the floor. I have never seen you look as beautiful as in that moment: untamed hair, happily playing in your underwear, having a conversation with Thomas the Tank Engine. There's a special kind of beauty that shines through from within when you're happy, when you're confident, when you're free. Eyeliner and a good blowout helps of course, but that glow, that light, that *je* ne *sais quoi*? That's where beauty comes from.

Confidence can't be taught—it's built, ounce by ounce, from within. Flattery is always great to hear, but it shouldn't be something you're dependent on for validation. I hope you will always know your own worth.

Danger

I have been impulsive and reckless too many times to count. You'll go through it too, thinking you're invincible. But, there's a difference between being brave and adventurous, and being careless and stupid. And sometimes, it's a fine line separating the two. There was the time a friend and I lost track of time painting the scenery high up on Inspiration Point in Yosemite. We were so in awe of the sunset, that we didn't realise darkness was setting in. As we ran down the poorly marked trail, I cut my leg, we heard bears growling, and took a few wrong turns before eventually making it back down safely. Having had enough of the woods after that harrowing experience, we abandoned our camping plans and drove all night straight to Vegas instead. Adventurous or careless?

Or the time Daddy and I walked back 20 minutes from a bar to our hostel at 2am through the dimly lit streets of Medellín—Escobar's hometown—just to save a couple of bucks? That one, definitely stupid. Or the time Masi and I drove through the narrow and maddening streets of Amman, where there were absolutely no traffic rules or marked lanes on the road. Adventurous? Yes, but next time, probably smarter to cab within the city, then drive out to Petra.

The lesson here isn't to avoid risk. It's to take a beat and think before you make your choices. You've always known what you wanted—it drove me crazy when you insisted on picking out all your own outfits even before your turned 2. As you grow up, there'll be many times you'll simply go with the flow, but my hope is that you will never allow yourself to feel pressured to go against your instincts. Don't rush. There's always a minute you can take to think before making a choice. And, always be brave enough to say "No" and have the courage to walk away.

Love and marriage

I have had my share of love: the young and idealistic, the fun and exciting, the passionate and crazy, the fleeting and superficial. And each one taught me something, and I left each one being more certain of what I wanted. And then, at a time when I least expected it, I met Daddy. He made me laugh, and there was this ease and openness wrapped up in excitement that I had never felt before. We both tried to ignore the fact that we were so obviously each other's "The One", but there was really no denying it. And here we are, 18 years later, and we still can't seem to get sick of each other no matter how much time we spend together. And he still makes me laugh. Every day.

Marrying the right person is one of the most important decisions you'll make in your life. I hope you choose well and end up with someone who is truly worthy of you, someone with whom you share the same outlook on life with, someone who complements you, who respects and values you, and someone who will love you through it all. The ubiquitous "Marry someone who loves you more than you love him" is possibly the worst advice ever. Nobody wins in that scenario.

However, along the way, there will be heartbreak. And what did I do when a boy broke my heart? I cried, listened to sad songs on repeat (I recall there being a lot Stevie Nicks, Toni Braxton and Joni Mitchell), cut my hair short, wrote letters I never mailed, and then cried some more on my best friend's shoulder. Aunty Liz has a freakish memory: she will tell you all the stories if you ask her. But, we all get through heartbreak, and years later, thank our lucky stars we did not end up with whats-his-name. Trust me. We all have different versions of this same story.

Family

There were many times I could've bought each of you your own ice cream, but bought a jumbo-sized one with three spoons instead. I could've set up separate art supplies for each of you to draw with, but instead put the whole set of markers in the middle. I made you take turns with your song requests in the car, work together to choose one book for story time, bunk together, cook together, play together, resolve many of your disagreements yourselves.

There may be oceans between you and your siblings in the future, and you may grow up being completely different from one another, and each have families of your own, but my hope is that you will always be able to depend on one another, make time to be together, and help each other make good decisions.

Struggles

We all have struggles: illness, heartbreak, abuse, loss, stress. We instinctively think, "Why me?", assuming we have been singled out somehow. Everyone has gone through struggles of their own, or will in their future. The important thing is how we get through it. Look for that silver lining and let that carry you to the other side—stronger, better and wiser. It is the moments that challenge us that give our life that depth, and help us empathise, and feel, and love.

At my lowest, I think of the shared experience every one of us on this planet has that bind us together as a human race. Of those orphans I met by the side of the river outside of Kigali, or the stories of a domestic helper who, as a child, used to be woken up by her father at 4am and kicked out, barefoot and scared, to beg for money on the streets of Mumbai so that he could squander it on liquor.

The life experiences you rack up help make up this huge storybook of your life. They help shape you, but do not let them define you. Holding on to anger, hurt, regret will stop you from experiencing so many new beautiful chapters. So allow yourself to feel each hurt, and most importantly learn from it, and eventually overcome it. Some life events you will never truly get over. And that's fine. But it will become part of a past you will revisit now and again, but don't let it write your future. And, in the event you find yourself face to face with someone so spiteful, step back and take the high road. Living well really is the best revenge.

Travel

Daddy and I are miles apart interests wise: he loves football, reading books on business, is a born entrepreneur, loves running. Pretty much everything I hate doing. I'd rather do cryptic crosswords, read a novel or a biography, and write. Though, we do like a lot of the same music and we both love a good movie.

But besides having the same outlook on life and how we want to live that life, the biggest thing we have in common is a love for travel—and the same type of travel. So when Daddy asked me if I'd rather go to Bora Bora for a week for our honeymoon or spend six weeks camping through East Africa—from Kenya and Tanzania, across to Rwanda, then down to Malawi, Zambia and Zimbabwe—it was the easiest choice I ever had to make. It was the same story when we dropped everything and backpacked for a year around Latin America in 2006.

There have been so many great travel tales, ones that were not packaged in some fabricated "authentic experience" tour, but ones where we actually made our own connections. We were there with the children in Oaxaca in 2006 during the teacher's strike; we grated coconuts and cooked freshly caught lobsters with the indigenous Kuna people on the San Blas islands (friends of our straight-out-of-Castaway Colombian boat captain). And then there was the time we powdered the whole town of Pasto (and everyone in it) with talc and snow-spray during the Carnaval de Negros y Blancos.

And there were the rough travel experiences. The time daddy and I were detained for four hours at Havana airport because they were convinced we were travelling on a fake passport, having never heard of Singapore. And the time our car was broken into in St Tropez and we lost not just money, phones and our passports, but tickets to the Madonna concert that weekend in Paris, and more importantly, our camera which had all our photos from that trip—the trip where Daddy proposed to me on a midnight stroll through the quaint French town of Etoges. There was the time in a cave in Semuc Champey where I almost drowned until a German guy in our group (well-equipped with a wetsuit and snorkel) helped me along. Or the Belize City daylight shakedown (travel tip: skip the city, head straight for the beautiful islands that they say inspired Madonna's *La Isla Bonita*). And the time my hands were all cut up from scrambling up sharp volcanic rocks in the dark, six feet away from the molten lava river of Volcán Papaya (while the pain was totally worth it, I definitely recommend gloves and a headlamp). I'm certain you'll go way past the 80-something countries Daddy and I have been to— the people in our family have lived everywhere from Aden to Zanzibar (yes, literally A to Z) and your ethnicity is another puzzle of at least a dozen pieces from around the globe. Travel is truly in your blood. I hope you take the time to enjoy and explore this beautiful planet.

Contentment

Daddy always tells me how I've taught him to live in the moment, to realise how very lucky we are to live this life we are living, to be surrounded by love and laughter each day, to have had all these opportunities. But, no one knows what the future holds. Life is cyclical, and there are bound to be highs and lows. The important thing is to have good people around you who will help carry you through the low points till you get over that rough patch. It's important to have ambition, to strive, to achieve goals you set for yourself—but while you're out chasing those dreams, don't forget to enjoy what (and who!) you have, right here, right now.

Decisions

Looking back, I see myself at so many crossroads that could've propelled my life in a whole other direction. Like the time I was so blinded by teenage love that I almost gave up my dream to go to the United States for college. But though my heart was resisting, my brain simultaneously kept pushing me to take my SATs, to research and apply to colleges, to finally make the decision I am so thankful I made.

Or the time Daddy and I almost gave up trying to have children after two consecutive heartbreaking miscarriages, but, with the encouragement of Dr Justine in Dubai, decided to try once more—and that changed our lives forever. I cannot imagine my life without you, and having you led to me becoming a mother of three! Anyone who knew Daddy and I 20 years ago would never have bet on that happening.

Or the time we decided to quit our jobs and backpack for one year, which led to so many amazing opportunities. New careers (and my realisation that I was meant to be a travel writer), amazing friendships (Uncle David who we met on that epic boat journey from Panama to Colombia along the infamous "drug route" ended up being the best man at our wedding), and of course, that special day that I was exhausted from a hike but decided to accept the impromptu dinner invite from Aunty Sharifah—the dinner where Daddy happened to sit next to me. The dinner that started it all.

Sometimes the small decisions you make in the spur of the moment lead you to the biggest moments of your life (like me deciding to accept a dinner invitation—showing up carrying a backpack and all). Those you can't really control. But the big ones, the ones you know deep inside are pivotal moments in your life, deserve a lot of thought. Hindsight is 20/20 they say, but as long as you make the best decision you can at the moment you have to make it, don't have any regrets.

Regret

What I've learned is that regret has to be the most useless emotion. It consumes you for hours, days, weeks and years on end. And until someone invents a time machine, nothing can undo what has been done. We all wish we would've spent more time with someone who is gone. Or not said something hurtful to someone we love. Or not made one decision over another. Once you've learned from it and know what you would do differently if in that situation again, let yourself let go of it. Forgive yourself.

Grief

If you're reading this, it's quite possible that I'm gone. And I know you must be hurting. In the darkest hours of my own childhood, when I missed my mother so much I couldn't breathe, I closed my eyes and imagined her laying next to me, hugging me tight and just listening as I poured my heart out.

But I want you to know that as cliché as it sounds, take it one step at a time. You somehow find strength from within you that you never knew existed. You are built with an inner strength and an inner fight for self-preservation. Your heart may be breaking, but your instincts and your mind with see you through even though it may not seem like you will ever recover. The pain cuts most on those big life milestones: your graduation, the day you get married to the person you love, the first time you hold your baby in your arms. But I will always be there, we are a part of each other, always remember my love. Half of me is you for always… the best part of me. My eyes are blinded with tears as I write this—I hope so much I am there for it all with you and that you can check off the rest of this list right now because we would've done it all by the time you read this. Otherwise, you guys complete it together, my darling, and I will live it through you.

Our bucket list

- Go wedding dress shopping together
- Drink pisco sours together after sandboarding in Ica
- Dance at a rock concert together
- Mother-daughter road trip!
- Play in the rain together
- Draw up a list of orphanages and commit to donate our time and money and make a difference
- Go for a Balinese massage together
- Teach you how to drive a stick shift (then pick out your first car together!)
- Compile our favourite recipes and start our own family cookbook
- Make a playlist for each other (mine's in this letter!)
- Get our nails and hair done together
- Movie marathon with our favourite movies growing up: Mine: *Dirty Dancing, Grease, Top Gun, Pretty Woman, The Breakfast Club, The Goonies, Cocktail.* Yours: *Wizard Of Oz, Charlie And The Chocolate Factory, Mamma Mia, Night At The Museum.*

- Help you get ready for your first date
- Go skydiving!

Finally, life

Some of the most amazing moments I've had are the ones that happened unexpectedly, thousands of miles away, and didn't cost a penny. Like the time we both lay in the sand under the Borneo sun watching a hundred baby turtles, blind and weak and with only their instincts to guide them, somehow find their way to the shoreline and go into the unknowing wide open dangerous ocean. And, after living a life of adventure and travel, return home, to start a new life. Trust your instincts and have confidence and faith in yourself and your decisions. Whether you realise it or not at the time, it will lead you to amazing heights, draw you towards inspiring people, guide you through your troubles, and pave a path towards a unique and beautiful life.

There's so much of your life story that remains unwritten— let it be a tale of love and adventure, and whenever you feel you're going off track, there's always room for a good plot twist to turn everything back around.

Every penny I've ever thrown in a fountain, every birthday candle I have blown out, every eyelash that I found on my cheek, every shooting star I've seen, I've wished for only one thing. Happiness. And it is all I wish for you, sweetheart.

With all my love for always,
Mummy

An adventurer at heart, **SHAAN MOLEDINA-LIM** has pitched a tent and camped in the middle of the Serengeti, had a near drowning experience in a Guatemalan cave, and steered a flooded yacht through a storm en route from San Blas to Cartagena. But that was all in a different life, before the arrival of her three beautiful children. Now, she often finds herself playing Genie to her kids—from fashioning pirate ships out of cardboard boxes to hosting weekly disco parties—though she does sneak in alone time to do cryptic crosswords, listen to Springsteen records, and plan trips. Shaan is a journalist by profession and has written for publications across Asia, including *The Straits Times*, *Vanilla*, *Mother&Baby*, and *Destinations Of The World News*. She is also the author of *If I could go anywhere in my dreams tonight...*, the first book of the four-part DREAM BIG! children's series.

Shaan and her family.

Everything I Want You To Be

Landy Chua

Dearest Tara, Amber and Nadia,

I want to begin by commending you on being fun partners on the adventures that Daddy and I have embarked on. It has been a series of hellos and goodbyes, with relocations crossing geographical and cultural boundaries, and you have taken the changes to homes and schools in your stride.

We have built our homes in Singapore, San Francisco, Hong Kong and Shanghai at some point in time. Tara changed six schools in four cities. Our first posting was when Tara was barely 4 years old. It took us four months to find a preschool for you, a 30-minute drive away. But you took to it like a duck to water.

The three of you have often been the odd ones out— you speak Mandarin but don't look Chinese. You speak English, but without an American or British accent. Most people find it hard to place you. You relied on your sincerity and open minds to make friends with people of all nationalities and to fit into the community. Even in the face of bullying, you admirably found strength to keep being yourself. In Hong Kong, Tara picked up Cantonese so that she could make friends with fellow dancers, who were not comfortable speaking English. Amber and Nadia took on the challenge of studying Chinese at native level in Shanghai. It was tough and lots of hard work. I know you are resilient girls, who are also adaptable and resourceful. We are so proud of you. Bravo!

Of our 13 years away from Singapore, my fondest memory is of our three-week road trip in the UK. You three shared a room and looked after each other. You managed your luggage bags independently. Each day, assembled at breakfast, you were ready to move on to the next destination. I saw you adhering to the schedule and looking out for each other, serving with your individual strengths. Tara, being stronger, carried the luggage; Amber was the time keeper, and Nadia scheduled the shower routine as you all shared one bathroom. I am glad to see that you have learnt the values of discipline and teamwork. I feel comforted that you will manage well in life.

As we settle back into life in Singapore, for how long I am not sure, you have applied yourself similarly to adapting to the local culture as a not-quite-local, just like you did with the other cities we have lived in. As typical Third Culture Kids, you have learnt the wisdom of observing before speaking, and respecting differences between people. I witness your encounters adapting to local ways and understanding your new circle of friends, and have seen you display maturity and wisdom. Be patient, my girls, give yourselves time, and soon you will be comfortable again.

In the blink of an eye, my firstborn has turned 18 and is ready for college. As you approach adulthood, I would like to share my life lessons and observations that I hope would prepare you better for life. I also want you to be equipped to live a life without me hovering over you. As a 6-year-old Tara once said: "Instinct is like a mummy inside of you telling you the right thing to do". I hope that you would have honed your "instincts" over the years which you can soon apply in your adult life.

Like most parents, what I want the most is for you to be good people and to be happy. I believe that we all have a desire to be good people. And I know we have often spoken about what makes a good person. I will try to condense our discussions through the years and put down some ideas to share with you.

Of all your grandparents, you have always had a special bond with your paternal Grandpa. So much so that you volunteered to come home during summer to cook for him when he was ailing. In our many conversations with him, Grandpa often spoke of the values of humility, integrity and hard work. So I shall begin with these.

Stay humble

No matter how many achievements you have clocked up, or how successful you become, stay humble. Everyone's journey can be heroic. For someone battling depression, just getting dressed and out the door is their heroic attempt at life. For some, walking into a new school as "the new girl" takes a lot of courage. And yet for others, they resuscitate people on the brink of death and bring them back to life. Be your own hero. Your Grandpa, during his career in the police force, cracked many commercial crime cases, recovering millions of dollars for companies. He was dubbed "The Million Dollar Cop" by the press. He received awards for his work in the police force, but he never bragged about his achievements. We only found out about the many people he had helped recently, at his funeral, when they came to pay their respects and shared anecdotes about him.

Strive to do the right thing

Sometimes it is difficult, oftentimes it is inconvenient. Integrity is non-negotiable. It sounds like a big, complicated idea. But it can be as simple as admitting your mistake. Or refusing to bow to the pressure to do something you think is not right. Always be fair and do right by yourself and others.

There is no replacement for hard work

Work for what you want, earn an honest living. While hard work now has a different definition from the days of physical labour, the value of working cannot be underestimated. Everyone should work, whether it is for money, satisfaction or love. Grandpa's long, illustrious career in the police force was not financially lucrative as defined by today's standards. Nevertheless, he gave his best effort and was determined to do a thorough job. For that, he received much recognition from his bosses and peers.

While I would like to paint a picture of an ideal world where all intentions are good and love is all around, I would also like to prepare you for the realities of life. Mankind is making strides towards equality for all, but we have not reached that goal yet. You will realise that discrimination exists and it can be through any measure—gender, age, race, car, even the schools you attended. I hope you know that you have the tools to overcome these shallow definitions that others may try to apply to you. No, you cannot change other people, but you can change the way you respond to them. As you know, I grew up in a working class home, but I was blessed with forward-thinking parents who encouraged me to dream and reach as high as I can. I have been an underdog for most of my life, and the following are my lessons and observations in my journey that I would like to share with you:

Be kind
Be kind to people, around you, regardless of their station in life. Whether it is the boss of the company, or the janitor in the building. Be kind because that is the person you are, not because they are more or less important than you. Be gracious in your interactions with them. Leave them better off for their encounter, no matter how brief, with you. A smile can go a long way and doesn't take much effort.

Help the less fortunate. Not everyone is born with the same resources. Some have more and some have less. Your charity efforts in Shanghai were signs of your leadership, initiative and kindness. I loved watching you perform for and interact with old folks, entertaining children from homes on an excursion and raising funds for heart operations for children who would otherwise have lost their lives. I am very proud of you. Keep up the good effort.

It is equally important to be kind to yourself. Don't be too harsh with yourself, we all make mistakes and we all fall short of our plans. Give yourself grace, pick yourself up, and try again. Life's journey is a marathon: stay the course and keep going.

Be brave

Dream big, and take action towards it. Let your dream be your guiding light by which you can channel your hard work and focus. Don't let life pass you by. Go chase that rainbow.

Venture into the unknown. One of my favourite quotes is from Andre Gide: "One does not find new lands without consenting to lose sight of the shore for a long time." Your dream is worth it. Leave that comfort zone and be prepared to work hard towards it. It is with this spirit that Daddy and I left Singapore to start our nomadic adventures, relocating wherever his job took us. We wanted to expand our horizons, and in the process, yours as well. The world is big, varied, and wonderful, and we wanted to explore all its mysteries with you.

Face your challenge head on. The problem will not go away, so take the bull by the horns and come up with a strategy to overcome it. Remember the night our home caught fire? We were standing barefoot outside the burning house with just the clothes on our backs, hugging each other. In a split second, our priorities became clear. The materials things we left behind in the house paled in comparison to the knowledge that all five of us were safe and unharmed. We would deal with replacing the things later. For the moment, we were safe together. In the days following the fire, we painstakingly cleared up the mess in the house and made a plan to pick up the pieces to resume our lives. It was weeks later before we could return to our home and life as we knew it. By then, we had renewed appreciation for the normal, and courage to know that we could face any problem together.

Be true

Be true to yourself. Know who you are, define yourself, and stay true to the core values that you hold dear. Study your strengths and weaknesses and work towards your goals. I chose to leave my career to raise my children. To me, it was the right thing to do for my family. I was the only one among my close friends to stay home with my child. Few understood why I would forego my career to look after my baby, when I could have easily outsourced it to grandparents or helper, as millions do. I was labelled lazy, unrealistic, wasteful, among other names. It was a lonely, misunderstood and confusing time, with all the noise surrounding what I thought was my decision. Sure, I paid a financial price, but in my opinion, my intangible rewards far, far outweigh the financial loss—I built the relationship I wanted with my children. And that, to me, is priceless.

Please know that this is by no means a suggestion that you follow my footsteps. Do what is right for you. Don't be swayed by peer pressure or pop culture. You are answerable to yourself and God. The only way you should be is the authentic you that God has created. Use His light to guide you.

Be heard

Speak up when you don't agree. Quoting the wise words of Mahatma Gandhi: "Be the change you want to see in the world." Take action if you want change. Write that letter, give suggestions. Be part of the solution. Don't fall into the trap of complaining but not taking action. I admire Amber's research and efforts at sustainability, living a minimalist life and reducing waste. Many drops make an ocean. Or in this case, every piece of plastic we keep out of the ocean (and landfill) counts.

Be courteous and respectful when voicing your point of view. That would gain you more audience than tantrums or hysterics would. Don't apologise for speaking up; don't apologise for not agreeing. Your opinion matters. You matter.

Be persistent

Many people have dreams, But what sets the successful apart is the persistence they apply to achieving their dreams. Keep improving, keep trying. In the words of Nelson Mandela, "The greatest glory in living lies not in never falling, but in rising every time we fall." So keep going—exercise that grit.

***

Next, I will address the second part of my wish for you: to be happy. "Happy" is such a broad concept, meaning different things to different people. What makes a person happy? For some it is material things, for others it is time with loved ones, and yet for others, it is to be "normal". What is your definition of happiness?

Remember that you are not your grades, you are not your clothing size, or even the size of your bank account. Know your worth. On this, I would like to quote Scripture: "So we fix our eyes not on what is seen, but on what is unseen,

Landy (centre) with her daughters, Tara, Nadia and Amber.

since what is seen is temporary, but what is unseen is eternal." 2 Corinthians 4:18

Know that in life, you will be hurt, you will feel frustrated and offended. But keep trying to be good anyway. I believe that our efforts to be good and do good bring with them happiness.

I hope that despite the busy-ness of life and the whirlwind of school, activities and friends, you will have learnt some principles that will see you through life. With the values that I have hoped to inculcate in you, and more importantly with God's blessings, may you find goodness and happiness in life.

With all my love,
Mum

LANDY CHUA is a mother to three spunky girls. She left a career in advertising and marketing to raise her children and to follow her husband on his career adventures in various cities. She embraced the nomadic lifestyle and added to her family in each city. In between, she kept herself busy designing a maternity fashion label, dabbling in direct marketing and organising events to raise funds for charity. She loves travelling, working out and a good bottle of wine. Not one to stay still, she is now cooking and baking to mixed reviews. Fortunately for her, her family is very forgiving of her cooking misadventures and continue to eat whatever she whips up in the kitchen.

How To Be Courageous

Jennifer Heng

Dear Alexis,

Your name means "defender of mankind".

Everyone said I was going to have a boy, but I knew you were a girl. Secretly, I researched girls' names, and I started from the letter "A". I loved how strong the name "Alexis" looked. When I saw what it meant, I knew that I was having an Alexis.

You've always been strong since you were an infant. Well, actually, even before you were born. You had strong arms and legs which you exercised a lot, especially in the last trimester. I wonder who you were defending. Maybe you were practising.

As a baby, you were strong both in body and will. You bounced back fast every time you fell sick. Daddy and I are grateful for that. You were also very strong-willed. Daddy and I sometimes didn't quite know how to deal with that.

No one could persuade you to eat those mushrooms. And those pink shoes with the blinking lights that Grandma wanted you to wear? There was no way they were going on your feet.

When I scolded you, you never cried right away. I could always see the strength in your eyes as you withheld your emotions, trying to remain strong, until you could not hold back any longer. It troubled me at times when you did that, but I was also relieved that you were not the kind who would unravel easily.

There was one word that we have used often on you: "fearless". You were about three when we brought you to the public swimming pool for the first time. You made a beeline for the pool and no one expected you to jump right in with a big smile on your face. Daddy and I sprinted into the pool after you, terrified. When we got hold of you, you were laughing your head off from excitement. You thought it was fun. We didn't.

We brought you to a theme park when you were a little older and there was a ride which turned out to be scarier than we expected. You didn't show any fear throughout the ride. But later that day, you told me that you didn't like it and that you were actually afraid of the sounds and darkness during the ride. I was surprised, because you didn't look afraid at all. I thought you were very brave.

I could go on about the things you did which sometimes impressed us, but other times would give us a near heart attack. To be honest, I rather enjoyed your sense of adventure. I loved how you took risks. I could see glimpses of courage and bravery. I love that about you, Alexis.

I know you don't often feel brave though. Remember that kindergarten concert you performed at? In the middle of the dance, your shoe fell off. My heart almost jumped out of my chest as I watched for what you would do. You picked up your shoe, skipped to your next position, placed the shoe in front of you and finished the dance with a big smile.

That night, you asked me, "Mama, what was your favourite part of the concert today?" I told you, "It was when you picked up your shoe, and continued dancing with a big smile. You know, sometimes in life, your dance partner falls sick and your shoe falls off, but you just have to smile and keep on dancing."

You replied, "I didn't like it, Mama. I was scared."

That, my dear Alexis, is courage. It is doing what you need to do, even when you are scared. You see, courage isn't the absence of fear. It is doing what you need to do, even when you are scared.

The other day, we watched *The Lord Of The Rings* together. Frodo and his friends were chased by monsters, betrayed by friends, fought in battles, shot by arrows and tempted by the power of the ring. They were overwhelmed by fear at times. Thankfully, they didn't give up, and eventually destroyed the ring. Such an inspiring example of courage!

I often imagine you standing up to speak against injustice, lies and oppression. One of my greatest desires is that you will rise up to the full purpose of what God has for you. I see you being a voice for the voiceless, a defender of the weak, a light in the darkness. This is not so that you can be admired by people, even though that may happen as well. It is so that people can see Jesus in you, and marvel at the greatness of God.

But when you need to defend something, you will definitely need courage. There will be enemies coming at you.

Your knees will feel like jelly and your heart will be pumping like mad. You will need to stand your ground to defend what is right, what is true and what is important. Your friends may run away. You may feel like running away. But Alexis, you will stand strong, not because you feel brave, but because you know that it is not your life you are protecting, but the lives of many others who are counting on you. It is not your strength that you are depending on, but the strength of God.

Courage is when you feel afraid, yet choose to act on what is right and good. Remember not to listen to your fear, but to have faith that doing the right thing is always better.

You told me that your friend once asked you to take that scented eraser from the bookstore without paying for it. You didn't do so, even though you really liked that eraser but didn't have enough pocket money for it. When I asked you why you didn't take it, you scrunched up your nose and said, "Woooowellll… I reeeeallyyyyy wanted to, but that's stealing."

I'm so proud of you. It takes courage to say no to something you really want but you know isn't right to have.

You know that I've always wanted to set up a centre to help pregnant women and save babies, right? You were very young when the first centre was set up. One of the mummies in the centre used to call you "Professor Alexis" because you went around, all of 3 years old, "supervising" the little babies in their cots. Everyone worked very hard to help the mummies, and it was wonderful because we saw their lives get better.

But we met with some problems. There were people who wanted to change the purpose of the centre. They offered me a lot of money to do what they wanted to do. They were not asking me to do a bad thing, but it wasn't what I had originally set out to do. It wasn't what I believed God had asked me to do.

I was very sad because I had to say no to them. As a result, we had to close the centre. You were 5 at that time, and couldn't quite understand why we couldn't go back to the centre anymore. It was such a difficult time for us, because it was like my dream died. I remember crying a lot, asking myself if I did the right thing.

I felt like a failure. Should I have been braver?

Years have passed and I can now look back and say that I don't regret the decision I made to stand my ground. Instead of thinking that I was not brave enough, I realised that it took courage to say no, to walk away from something which was not what God intended for. I had thought that I was weak because I didn't try to "fight back". But now I realise that sometimes it takes more courage to walk away.

There will be times in our lives when we will be tempted to do things which are not what God wants us to do. Some of these things may even seem good. People will say, "What's wrong with this?" But have courage to say no to those things. Have courage to withstand the pressure from those around you. At the end of the day, remember that we are responsible for our own decisions, so choose well.

Anyway, now we have Safe Place. I'm so glad it's going well. I love that you are so much a part of the work and want to be on staff when you're older. You'll have to study hard and get the right qualifications to apply for a job at Safe Place, okay? You're not going to get the job just because you are the founder's daughter.

Many people thank me for Safe Place and tell me they are inspired by what we're doing. The truth is, I'm inspired constantly by the brave mummies that we meet at Safe Place.

Auntie V's family kicked her out of her home when they found out she was pregnant before marriage. She was so afraid and hurt that she wanted to abort her baby so that she can go back home and live like nothing has happened. But when she saw the beating heart of her baby during the ultrasound, she told us, "This is my baby. I can't possibly have an abortion. This is a life." Courageously, she decided to raise her child as a single mother. Even though her family still doesn't accept her, she hopes that she can one day bring her baby to visit his grandparents. Auntie V knew that she should not have gotten into a relationship with her ex-boyfriend who abandoned her. Instead of blaming it on others, she decided to take responsibility and do the right thing.

Two months ago, we helped Auntie M's baby move to his adoptive family. Auntie M knew that she wasn't able to raise her baby on her own when she found out she was pregnant. She cried and cried when she decided to place her baby for adoption. I think mummies who place their babies for adoption are the bravest people on earth. To carry your baby for nine months in your womb, go through painful labour to give birth, and eventually release your baby to grow up in another family is one of the hardest things anyone can do. I admire Auntie M so much. Even at her young age, she knew that the best thing she could do for her baby was to have him be part of a family that would be able to raise him well. People may say she's irresponsible for abandoning her baby. I say no—she has done a noble and courageous thing. She laid aside her own pain and selfish desires, and did what was best for her baby.

We still cry when we think about Auntie M and her baby. But we know that she has done an amazing thing, and the baby and his new family are doing well.

There are so many stories of brave mummies who have made difficult, painful decisions so that they can do the right thing. They faced rejection, anger and discrimination, sometimes from their closest loved ones. In spite of that, many of them courageously try again and again, one day at a time, to get better, to get stronger, for the sake of their child.

I read a quote by Mary Anne Radmacher that says, "Courage doesn't always roar. Sometimes courage is the little voice at the end of the day that says, 'I'll try again tomorrow.'"

We may admire people who are on stage, or in the news for doing courageous things. They are heroes whom we applaude and admire. While that's wonderful, remember that courage is not always what you see in the spotlight. Sometimes it's in the little unseen things that courage is needed.

Unseen things such as forgiveness, admitting that you are wrong, and being humble. The other day, you were angry with me because I broke our "no screen time after dinner" rule. Even after I said sorry, you couldn't forgive me. I was very sad because I didn't know what else to do. It took courage for me to admit my mistake.

You were mad at me all night but you forgave me the next day. I knew that it took great courage for you to forgive me because you were mad at me for so long! (Usually you forgive me like, five minutes later.) I knew how upset I made you and I was glad that we worked out this little but important episode in our lives. Admitting we are wrong and forgiving others, both require courage.

Speaking about that, do you know that Daddy is one of the bravest people I know? He's usually the first to say sorry when we argue. You also know that if it wasn't for Daddy's courageous love for me, I wouldn't have been able to write my book and share my story publicly.

That wasn't easy. When I was writing my book, I was afraid of what people would think of Daddy. He didn't do anything wrong, so I didn't want anyone to think bad of him. I worried about his reputation and if people would say bad things about him for marrying someone with a past like mine.

But Daddy was amazing. He championed me all the way, and was always the one who encouraged me to tell my story, and to do what God has placed in my heart. He never worried for himself, but constantly assured me that we are in this together.

Over the years, Daddy continues to be my greatest champion and cheerleader. My book *Walking Out Of Secret Shame*, Dayspring New Life Centre, Good Gifts City Church and Safe Place would never have happened if it wasn't for Daddy's support and strength. I always think that he doesn't get enough credit for his part in all these things, because I'm usually the one that gets the attention. So Alexis, remember that I have been able do what I have because of Daddy's courage and love for you and me. I hope in future, you will meet a man with that same courage and love.

There is just one last thing I need to say about courage, and it's also the most important thing.

When my book was published, many people told me how inspired and blessed they were by it. The most common thing I heard was, "You're so brave! Thank you for sharing your life this way! You're so brave for telling your story!"

Honestly, I didn't think I was brave. In fact, I was really scared when I was writing my book. I was afraid of what other people would think about me. Brave was definitely not a word I would use to describe myself.

But if it wasn't because I was brave, then what was it that made me write the book? I thought about it for a while, and one day, I got the answer.

I wrote the book not because I was brave, but because I was free. Free from my past. Free from the guilt and shame that once held me prisoner. It wasn't my courage that led me to write the book. It was my freedom. The one I found in Jesus Christ.

That, Alexis, is the most important thing. The most courageous thing I have ever done, and am still doing, is following Jesus. Because I have freedom in Him, I can be brave and courageous and do anything He asks.

So: Be courageous when you feel afraid but still choose to do the right thing. Be courageous when you need to say no when everyone else says yes. Be courageous when you face difficulties and feel like giving up. And always, always be courageous when following Jesus.

Proud of you always,
Mama

JENNIFER HENG tells her inspiring life story in her book *Walking Out Of Secret Shame*. A passionate advocate of building a culture of life in Singapore and Asia, she is currently the Director of Safe Place, an initiative to empower women with unsupported pregnancies to make life-giving choices. In 2015, she was named "Most Inspiring Woman - Great Women of Our Time" by *Singapore Women's Weekly*. She was also one of "Ten Outstanding Young Persons of the World" in Singapore that year. She speaks regularly in schools, conferences, organisations and the prisons. Most of her professional career was spent in non-profit organisations in the areas of the arts, religion and social impact. She's married with one daughter, loves spicy food and dreams of travelling to Antarctica one day.

Jennifer and Alexis.

Lessons In Love And Life

Yen Chua

My dearest daughters Choden and Chodze,

Two decades ago, I was approaching 30 and had decided to be single. I was doing research for my Master's thesis at the National Institute of Education and had to travel to India to interview a few Tibetan Buddhist masters.

That was when I met your father. He was working as a secretary for a respected Buddhist teacher. Whenever there were guests from overseas, these teachers would send their driver to receive them from the train station. But somehow the driver was unavailable that day, so they sent your father.

He was a friendly and chatty guy, while I was shy and quiet person. He liked me but I didn't like him. I spent a month in India. As I was alone, it was very kind of him to take me to some lovely cafes to have Tibetan food as I was having jaundice from eating too much spices and ghee. The cafe was called Lhasa Restaurant (years later, your father and I would embark on a pilgrimage to Tibet and stay in Lhasa.

That was his first trip back to his homeland, as he was born in India after his parents escaped from Tibet during the Chinese Communist invasion).

There is a river near the Buddhist teacher's palace in Dehradun where locals would go for a swim or take their clothes to wash. So your father took me, together with his friends that had come to visit from Delhi on Vespa scooters to spend the afternoon there. He was squatting on a huge rock and washing his clothes and socks—that was the moment I fell for him. I thought to myself, "This man is really down-to-earth, carefree and totally unpretentious." I felt a simple happiness just being with him.

We were married the next year and he moved to Singapore. When he arrived, he had only a cabin-sized suitcase. Now, we have an apartment, the two of you and your little brother.

You know your Mommy prefers to paint than to write, but I would like to leave you some words and art that I hope you will always hold in your heart.

Choden (your name means "blessed with Dharma" in Tibetan), you made me a mother in 2008 and from that moment, I discovered the person I really was, that I had never known was inside me all along. Then you came along, Chodze (your name means "to perform Dharma activities") and I found out that my heart has the ability to grow larger and feel more, more than I ever thought possible. When your little brother came, a huge surprise, two years ago, motherhood was cemented as a core element of me.

I have three things I need to leave with you, because I want you both to grow up and become the very special women that you are meant to be. Life is not always easy—sometimes it is full of pain. But sometimes pain can be a stepping stone to great happiness.

ONE: Be brave to say "no" if it doesn't feel or seem right

I was abused as a child until I was a young adult. After 16 years of physical violence, I suffered emotional abuse for another two decades before I said, enough was enough.

I walked away from my abuser a few years after I gave birth to both of you. It took a lot of courage for me to say "No". When I read about young girls that report that they have been abused, I know it has cost them all the courage they have inside them, because most of the time, the abuser is a caregiver, a person a child looks up to from the moment he or she was born.

When the police came, I decided not to press charges, because I did not want her to go to jail.

But this is what I want to say: Abuse is never okay, no matter who it comes from. Your father and I have raised you both with as much love as we could fill our home, but you may—you will—meet people in your life who will try to abuse you. It is not okay. Walk away, and if you can't, get help. I will be here to help you as long as I live. Seek help, find healing—you are not what happens to you.

TWO: Be kind always

Remember that you are the difference to this world. One word of kindness from you can change somebody's life.

Choden, a few years ago, you received $200 when you won the Edusave Character Award. You then decided to donate the money to your school. Your Daddy and I were so pleased by your generous decision, and our hope for you is that you continue to be the best you can, to serve society and help the needy.

Chodze, I remember when you were 7 and we were walking to the train station when, along the way, we heard and saw a girl stomping on some flowers and shouting, "Step, step, step on the flowers until they die!" I was shocked by her behaviour, but you walked up to the girl and held her hand. You tried to calm her down and you told her to stop

The Mother, *September 2017. Acrylic ink and charcoal on canvas, 61 cm x 61 cm.*

doing that, and the girl did stop. I was so comforted that you took the matter into your own hands and were able to resolve it gently.

Blessed Nicolas Barré once said, 'The gifts given to you are for others'. Remember that power you have to bring healing to this world, to others.

和你, *2017. Japanese ink on watercolour paper, 50 cm x 150 cm.*

THREE: Mommy won't be here forever

I love you girls so much. You both are unusual children, so loving and intuitive. Choden, you once told me that you will work hard and become a teacher, and earn a lot of money so that I won't have to work and I can paint full-time. I love you so much for loving me.

Chodze, you once told me that although enlightenment is "cool", you don't want to be separated from Mommy, because you would be very sad if we can't be together and if you can never see me again.

But the truth is, Mommy won't be here forever. That is a fact of life. But my hope is that you will grow up to be wonderful mommies to wonderful children, just like you are to me now.

Let's capture every moment, let's enjoy one another's company and love for as long as we live. Let's make every day count. Thank you for giving me a chance to be a mother and a better person. I love you all, always.

Love,
Mommy

YEN CHUA is an artist, art therapist and educator. She has a BFA from the San Francisco Art Institute, a Diploma in Chinese Painting from the Beijing Central Academy of Fine Arts, and MA (Research) from the National Institute of Education in Singapore, and an MA in Art Therapy from the LASALLE College of the Arts, Singapore. Yen has exhibited globally, and is widely recognised for her ability to express deep emotions through the mythical, magical worlds and beings she creates. Yen has been happily married for 18 years and is the proud mother of two daughters, aged 12 and 10, and a son, aged 2.

Yen and her daughters, Choden and Chodze.

ALSO AVAILABLE

Letter to my Son

*Words of wisdom, advice and
lessons on life from parents*

EDITED BY FELIX CHEONG

FEATURING CONTRIBUTIONS BY
Anita Devi Pillai, Anthony Goh, P N Balji,
Bernard Harrison, Chris Henson, Christopher Ng,
Clement Mesanas, Daniel Yap, Darren Soh, Dinesh Rai,
Fong Hoe Fang, Gilbert Koh, Kenny Chan, Lester Kok,
Mark Laudi, Nizam Ismail, Olivier Ahmad Castaignede,
Roland Koh, Sanjay Kuttan, Vicky Chong